I0158812

TM 9-2900

WAR DEPARTMENT

TECHNICAL MANUAL

MILITARY EXPLOSIVES

DISCLAIMER:

This manual is sold for historic research purposes only, as an entertainment. It contains obsolete information and is not intended to be used as part of an actual operation of maintenance training program. No book can substitute for proper training by an authorized instructor.

©2022 Periscope Film LLC
All Rights Reserved
978-1-940453-69-9
www.PeriscopeFilm.com

TECHNICAL MANUAL }
No. 9-2900 }

WAR DEPARTMENT,
WASHINGTON, *August 29, 1940*.

# MILITARY EXPLOSIVES

Prepared under direction of the
Chief of Ordnance

Chapter 1. Propellants.                                          Paragraphs
    Section I. General_____ 1-5
           II. Manufacture of smokeless powder_____ 6-17
          III. Granulation of smokeless powder_____ 18-20
           IV. Stability and storage of smokeless powder___ 21-26
            V. Inspection of smokeless powder_____ 27-31
           VI. Compound propellants_____ 32-34
          VII. Black powder_____ 35-39
Chapter 2. Military High Explosives.
    Section I. General_____ 40-41
           II. Trinitrotoluene (TNT)_____ 42-49
          III. Ammonium picrate (Explosive D)_____ 50-55
           IV. Picric acid_____ 56-61
            V. Nitrostarch explosives_____ 62-67
           VI. Tetryl_____ 68-73
          VII. Mercury fulminate_____ 74-79
         VIII. Amatol_____ 80-83
           IX. Lead azide_____ 84-88
Chapter 3. Bibliography_____ 89

CHAPTER 1

# PROPELLANTS

SECTION I

# GENERAL

                                                              Paragraph
Definitions _____ 1
Classification_____ 2
Action_____ 3
Use_____ 4
Composition_____ 5

1. **Definitions.**—*a. Explosive.*—An explosive may be defined in general as being a gaseous, a liquid, or a solid substance, or mixture

---

*This manual supersedes War Department Document No. 947, August 14, 1919.

of substances, which upon application of a blow to a small portion of its mass, or by a rise in temperature is converted in a small space of time into other substances more stable which are mainly gases or vapors but may include solids. The chemical changes thus produced develop a sudden rise in pressure in the surrounding medium, and the word "explosive" is applied as a general term to the different types of phenomena occurring in this sort of reaction. Coincident with this evolution of gas a considerable amount of heat is evolved which produces a flame. A high explosive is one in which this change occurs within the shortest space of time and the phenomenon accompanying this decomposition is termed a detonation. Detonation therefore applies more properly to the chemical reaction incident to the almost instantaneous decomposition of the high explosive. However, it is not properly employed when discussing the analogous reaction incident to combustion of a slower burning explosive as smokeless powder. The general term explosive which finds universal acceptance applies alike to high explosives, black powder, and smokeless powder. It will be seen therefore that the accepted distinction between the different classes of explosives is based primarily upon their relative speed of decomposition, and only those explosives are classified as high explosives in which this chemical change is considered practically instantaneous.

*b. Explosion.*—Marshall (see par. 89) defines an explosion thus: "When gas or vapor is released so suddenly as to cause a loud noise an explosion is said to take place as, for instance, the explosion of a steam boiler or of a cylinder of compressed gas." The barrel of the gun may be considered at the time of the explosion as being a cylinder of compressed gas. Walls of the gun constitute walls of the cylinder, the breech mechanism one end, and the projectile the other.

**2. Classification.**—Berthelot (see par. 89) enumerates and distinguishes between eight different groups of explosive bodies which owe their transformation either to application of some external circumstance such as fire, shock, friction, or else to aid of a secondary reagent or chemical agent which propagates within itself an explosive wave and finally accomplishes a general explosion. Of these eight groups the greater number of military explosives fall within the third, fourth, and eighth divisions:

*a. Explosive inorganic compounds.*—Definite bodies, liquids or solids, as azides.

*b. Explosive organic compounds.*—Definite bodies, liquids or solids, in which classification occurs the nitrated derivatives of the carbohydrates as nitrocellulose, nitrostarch, and the nitrated derivatives of the aromatic compounds as trinitrotoluene (TNT).

*c. Mixtures.*—Mixtures formed by oxidizable and oxidizing bodies, solid or liquid, neither of these being explosives separately as, for instance, black powder, etc.

**3. Action.**—If an explosive were used which gave instantaneous detonation the force so generated would either burst the barrel of the gun or else (in the case of a reduced charge) would not impart sufficient velocity to the projectile to develop maximum efficiency. This particular point illustrates the necessity of using a relatively slow burning explosive as the means of propelling the projectile from the muzzle of the gun, an explosive which may be designated as the propelling charge or propellant. Compression in the powder chamber of the gun must be developed slowly at first, gradually increasing in intensity until the projectile in the case of the ideal gun is forced to the muzzle, at which place the maximum pressure of the charge is exerted. However, in actual practice the maximum compression in the gun is never developed at the muzzle, a condition which would cause bursting according to our present design in which maximum pressure is exerted just after the projectile starts moving from its original position; usually maximum pressure occurs when the projectile is only 1 foot or so ahead of its original position. In this function of projecting a shot, the high explosive as such finds no application. However, it may occur as a constituent of a propellant as for example, nitroglycerin, a high explosive which is an ingredient of certain sporting, pistol, and cordite powders. The field of usefulness of the high explosive as a class is quite different and advantage is taken of its properties of detonation to use it within the shell or other bursting projectile so that at the proper time the shell will be disrupted through detonation of the high explosive with which it was filled.

**4. Use.**—The present tendency is to draw a sharp distinction between two classes of explosive bodies in accordance with the use to which they are put and also in accordance with the speed of reaction whereby combustion or decomposition takes place.

*a. Propellants.*—Those substances or mixtures whose rate of combustion is such as to permit their use for propelling projectiles from guns are termed propellants.

*b. High explosives.*—Those substances whose rate of decomposition is so very high as to preclude their use as propellants but which on the other hand bring about very powerful disruptive action are known as detonating explosives, disruptives, or more commonly, as high explosives.

**5. Composition.**—*a.* The different substances used for high explosives are very many, but at the present time one substance with certain modifications and additions is used as the base of the propelling charge. This substance is a colloid formed by action of a solvent upon a nitrated cellulose with or without addition of nitroglycerin, and in its final form is called "smokeless powder."

*b.* Selection of these various substances is dependent upon their cheapness of manufacture and their safety in handling. In order that these data may be evaluated properly it is necessary that the following properties and measurements be determined:

(1) Chemical equation involved in change of substance from liquid or solid to gaseous state.

(2) Thermo-chemical values as given in heats of formation of the different components.

(3) Specific heats.

(4) Densities.

(5) Relative pressure which may be developed by comparing equal parts of a new explosive with that of one well known.

(6) Type and amount of energy required to initiate reaction.

(7) Rapidity of reaction.

(8) Relative power of the explosive.

SECTION II

## MANUFACTURE OF SMOKELESS POWDER

|  | Paragraph |
|---|---|
| Historical sketch | 6 |
| Term and form | 7 |
| Manufacturing processes | 8 |
| Purification of raw cotton | 9 |
| Nitration | 10 |
| Purification of pyrocotton | 11 |
| Formation of colloid | 12 |
| Graining and cutting | 13 |
| Solvent recovery | 14 |
| Drying | 15 |
| Blending | 16 |
| FNH and NH powders for cannon | 17 |

**6. Historical sketch.**—The first nitrocotton which was made was the result of an experiment performed in 1838, when Pélouze observed the action of nitric acid upon cotton. A few years later in 1845, Schönbein realized the importance of this material as an explosive and developed it to such a point that he endeavored to sell the product to various governments. However, early attempts at the use of this new explosive, especially in Austria-Hungary, were fraught with disaster, for factories were destroyed and guns were damaged as a result of unfamiliarity with chemical and physical properties of this new substance.

However, the unfortunate experiences of the Austrians did not deter the English chemists from developing the industry. Prominent among these men at this time was Sir Frederick Abel who started a small factory for the manufacture of nitrocotton at Waltham Abbey. The industry received tremendous support, and the important progress which was made during the next few years was in fact responsible for the later developments of collodion-photography and for the artificial silk industry.

During this period use of guncotton as an explosive was restricted entirely to blasting purposes. In seeking a new material which might be used in place of black powder and which would not have the objectionable features of the old propellant such as smoke, residue, etc., it occurred to Schultze that guncotton would be a possible substitute for this purpose. Experiments were made with many different substances and compounds but the first ones to achieve any notable success were the Schultze and the E. C. powders. These won instant recognition as shotgun powders but proved too quick for use in rifled arms.

About the year 1886, another important step in development of smokeless powder was made by Vieille, a French chemist. He incorporated nitrocotton with a mixture of ether and alcohol, and rolled the resulting paste, a colloid, into thin sheets which were cut into small squares and dried. Contemporaneous with this work, Nobel developed ballistite, a powder obtained by gelatinizing a low-nitrated nitrocotton with nitroglycerin. Shortly after this, a modification of ballistite known as cordite was adopted as a smokeless powder. This propellant consisted of a mixture of high-nitrated guncotton gelatinized by means of acetone. In this mixture nitroglycerin and vaseline were incorporated.

At the present time all nations use as a propellant either gelatinized nitrocotton alone or else gelatinized nitrocotton mixed with varying quantities of nitroglycerin.

**7. Term and form.**—*a. Application of term.*—The term "smokeless powder" when considered from the exact meaning of the word is a paradoxical misnomer, for the substance is not entirely smokeless and it is not a powder.

*b. Form.*—Smokeless powder is manufactured in the form of small flakes, strips, pellets, sheets, or perforated cylindrical grains. The last-mentioned form of grain is the one most commonly used in the military powders manufactured in the United States. These cylindrical grains are made with diameters varying from 0.032 inch for the cal. .30 rifle to 0.947 inch for the 16-inch gun, and in corresponding lengths varying from 0.085 inch to 2.170 inches. In general, the smaller caliber weapons are provided with cylindrical powders having a single perforation running lengthwise through the grain, while powders having seven perforations are used in the larger caliber weapons. Triperforated powders have been used experimentally and a rosette or so-called sliverless grain has been used to some extent; such forms of grains are resorted to only when special ballistic properties are required.

**8. Manufacturing processes.**—The different processes incident to manufacture of pyro smokeless powder may be summarized under the following heads:

*a.* Purification and mechanical preparation of raw cotton. This includes picking and drying processes.

*b.* Nitration of cotton. This is accomplished by treating the cotton with a mixture of nitric and sulphuric acid, thus producing a cellulose nitrate or "pyrocotton."

*c.* Purification of pyrocotton from all traces of free acids and lower nitrates.

*d.* Mixing of pyrocotton with ether-alcohol and pressing to form a colloid.

*e.* Granulating of the powder by pressing the colloid through steel dies.

*f.* Final processes of solvent recovery, drying, and blending.

*g.* The order of the various steps in the manufacturing processes for nitrocellulose and for pyro powder are shown in figure 1 and details of the various manufacturing procedures are outlined below.

**9. Purification of raw cotton.**—*a.* (1) *Process.*—The cotton used in manufacture of smokeless powder is usually *linters*, although other grades of cotton and wood pulp may be used. The charge of raw cotton is cooked in a digester for about 6 hours with a solution of approximately 2 percent caustic soda. The digestion is carried out under a pressure of about 72 pounds per square inch which corresponds to a temperature of 152° C. After removing the spent caustic liquors by washing, the cotton is treated with a solution of commercial bleaching powder of about 2½ percent strength. This bleaching is carried out at 36° C., and as short a time as is necessary

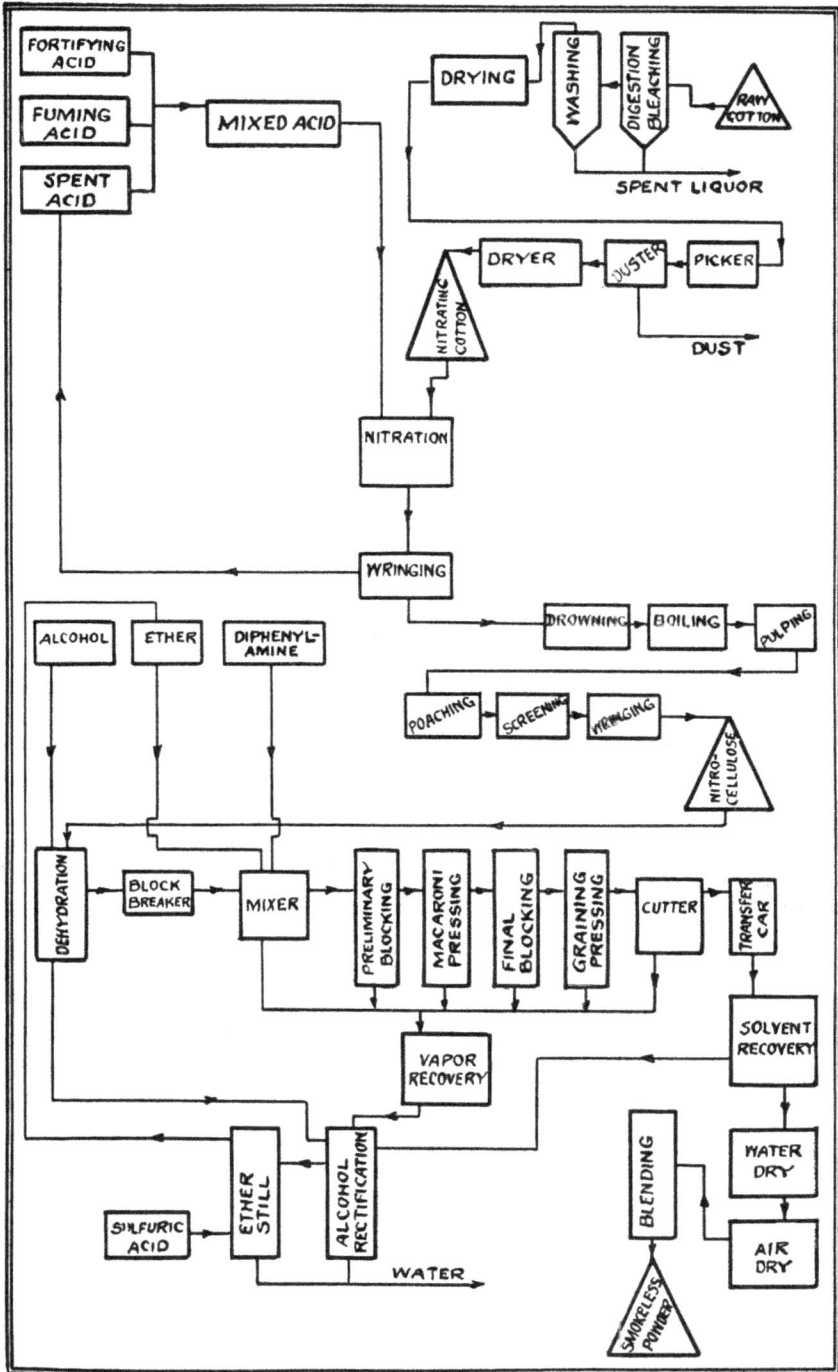

FIGURE 1.—Flow sheet for manufacture of smokeless powder.

to decolorize the fibers is employed. The excess bleach is destroyed by addition of a small quantity of sulphuric acid. The charge is then washed free of bleaching agents and dried.

(2) *Object*.—The object of boiling with soda and the bleaching treatment is to reduce the content of vegetable oil, resinous material, and other extractible substances. It is very important that the alkaline treatment should not be excessive and that the cotton should not be overbleached, otherwise the contents of hydrocellulose and oxycellulose will be undesirably high, as indicated by the test for alkali soluble described in the specification for cellulose (U. S. Army Specification No. 50–11–44).

*b. Picking*.—If uniform nitration is to be obtained it is essential that the cotton be of uniform low moisture content, of uniform physical condition, and that it be free from lumps or any extraneous material. To obtain this uniformity the cotton is put through a picking machine of which there are various forms. One of these machines is provided with a toothed roller which engages the cotton as it is moving along the feeding table and carries it into such a position that it is caught and torn apart by rows of sharp hook-shaped teeth set along six evenly spaced elements of a skeleton cylinder revolving at the rate of 1,000 revolutions per minute. This operation reduces the cotton to a fluffy state after which it is caught and blown by an air blast into a large flue leading into the drying room. At one portion of its journey through the flue the cotton passes through a machine which comprises a system of W-shaped flues containing a set of baffles in the form of prongs which serve to fluff out the cotton and separate the fibers from the heavy dust. This dust settles to the bottom of bends in the flues whence it is removed. From this machine the cotton is blown into the dry house.

*c. Drying*.—(1) Two systems of drying are in use, one, the continuous drier in which the cotton is conveyed by a belt through a long chamber heated to about 100° C., the other by placing the cotton in a large chamber which is heated by hot air blast. The former is a continuous operation and the cotton issuing from the drier is weighed directly into metal containers and transferred to the nitrating house. Entering cotton usually contains about 8 percent moisure. Treatment reduces this to approximately 0.5 percent.

(2) The chamber system is the more expensive of the two and the least desirable from the standpoint of time. These chambers are of such a size as to hold approximately 2,500 pounds of cotton. After the chamber has been filled, it is closed tightly and the heat is gradually raised until the temperature reaches 105° C., where it is held

for 24 hours. After a laboratory test of the cotton has shown less than 1 percent of moisure, the dried cotton is weighed in lots of 32 pounds in closed fiber containers which are transferred to the nitrating house by means of a telpherage system.

10. **Nitration.**—In nitration of cellulose there are two reactions to be considered from the manufacturing standpoint. Although these reactions occur simultaneously, for the sake of clearness in description they are to be considered separately. First, formation of the nitric acid ester of cellulose, and subsequent removal of water formed in the reaction by sulphuric acid.

*a. Acids.*—There are three kinds of acid used in nitrating, namely, fortifying, fuming sulphuric, and spent acid. The spent acid is that which is recovered after nitration has been completed. This acid is built up or fortified by use of a fortifying acid having a strength of approximately 50 to 55 percent nitric and 50 to 45 percent sulphuric. This acid supplies all of the nitric acid necessary for new nitration and a portion of the sulphuric acid. The rest of the sulphuric acid is supplied by adding fuming acid of 104 percent $H_2SO_4$. The main function of the sulphuric acid is to combine with water formed during reaction, and in this manner to prevent dilution of the nitric acid. At the present time mixing of mixed nitrating acids is generally accomplished by agitation with iron paddles rather than by use of compressed air.

*b. Systems.*—Four different systems of nitration have been used in this country, the DuPont mechanical-dipper process, the centrifugal process, the Thompson displacement system, and the pot process. The mechanical-dipper process has practically displaced the other processes in this country. The relative proportions of the nitric acid, sulphuric acid, and water vary not only with the different processes, but also with change in weather conditions, more particularly of temperature. The sulphuric acid content is maintained very nearly constant, and the variation in nitric acid is less than 1 percent and is largely accounted for by the fact that a certain amount of denitration of nitrocotton takes place during warm weather. Unless the nitric acid is increased to take care of this phenomenon, the resulting nitrocellulose will be below specification requirements for nitrogen content.

(1) *Du Pont mechanical-dipper process.*—(*a*) The entire cycle of operation in this process is not more than 35 minutes. Under ordinary working conditions the fumes are negligible, whereas in all the other nitrating systems the fumes are always in evidence so that from the standpoint of health of operatives this system is much to be preferred, provided that proper care is always exercised in manipulation of the machinery.

(b) A nitrating unit in this system consists of a battery of four iron or stainless-steel nitrators so situated that they can all be handled from a central point. In each nitrator are two vertical revolving paddles operated in opposite directions from each other, the motion being from without inward. These paddles consist of a series of horizontal arms so placed upon the post that when set in motion the cotton is quickly drawn beneath the surface of the acid. A charge of approximately 1,500 pounds of acid having a temperature of 30° C. is used in each nitrator of which the following is a fair average composition: $HNO_3$, 21 percent; $H_2SO_4$, 63 percent; $N_2O_4$, 0.5 percent; $H_2O$, 15.5 percent.

FIGURE 2.—DuPont mechanical-dipper process, nitration floor, Carney's Point, N. J.

(c) When the acid has been run in, the paddles are set in motion and about 32 pounds of cotton added. The speed of these paddles is approximately 60 revolutions per minute. Nitration is continued for 24 minutes, after which the bottom discharge valve is then opened and the nitrocotton and acid dropped rapidly into a centrifugal wringer located below the nitrator unit. This centrifugal wringer rotates slowly at first at about 300 revolutions per minute until the whole charge is in the centrifuge. The speed of the wringer is then increased to about 1,100 revolutions per minute and held at this rate for 3½ minutes. The spent acid is run by gravity from the outer jacket of the wringer into catch tanks where small amounts of nitrocellulose settle out. The spent acid runs from these catch tanks to a blow case, and is either blown into mixing tanks or any surplus spent acid set aside for denitration or other means of disposal.

(*d*) The nitrated cotton obtained is forked through a bottom discharge of the centrifuge into an immersion basin below. As fast as the nitrated cotton falls into the basin it is submerged by a heavy stream of water distributed by fishtail or other form which combines the greatest dispersion of water with the maximum force for submersion.

(*e*) The pyrocotton, as it is now called, is next transferred by means of pumps or by gravity to the boiling tub house.

FIGURE 3.—DuPont mechanical-dipper process, wringing centrifugal floor, Picatinny Arsenal, N. J.

(2) *Centrifugal process.*—In this system the nitrating and the separation of the spent acid from the nitrated cotton are both carried on in a large nitrating centrifugal. The latter is filled with a definite amount of the mixed acid, usually 50 times the weight of the cotton charge, at a temperature of about 32° C., the weighed charge of cotton (usually 30 pounds) immersed rapidly by means of an iron fork and allowed to stand for about 20 minutes, with occasional turning over by means of the fork. The drain cock is then opened

11

and the spent acid separated by centrifuging, after which the charge
is forked out and drowned as in the mechanical-dipper process.

(3) *Pot process.*—(*a*) In the pot process the nitration is best carried out in iron pots. These are filled with the mixed acid, the cotton
immersed and allowed to digest for 20 to 30 minutes when the entire
contents are dumped into a centrifugal wringer. The pots are moved
and dumped by means of a suitable two-wheeled truck conveyer. The
pot process employs considerably less acid than the centrifugal proc-

FIGURE 4.—DuPont mechanical-dipper process, immersing basin and exit flume floor,
Picatinny Arsenal, N. J.

ess, about 35 parts of acid being sufficient to cover the cotton properly.

(*b*) The charge of cotton used is generally about 4 pounds. Sometimes much smaller pots made of earthenware are used holding a
charge of only 2 pounds of cotton, several of these charges constituting a wringer charge. These small pots are usually emptied by hand.

(*c*) The spent acid recovered from the centrifugals is transferred
to storage tanks to be fortified, as has already been mentioned. Its
average composition is approximately $HNO_3$, 18 percent; $H_2SO_4$, 65
percent; $N_2O_4$, 0.5 percent; $H_2O$, 16.5 percent.

*c. Cellulose.*—(1) The exact molecular weight of cellulose is not known; however, the empirical formula of cellulose is assumed to be $(C_6H_{10}O_5)_x$, and it is thus discussed by Marshall as follows:

At first the simplest possible formula was assumed for cellulose, $C_6H_{10}O_5$, and guncotton of high nitrogen content and low solubility in ether-alcohol was supposed to be formed by the substitution of three $NO_2$ groups for hydrogen atoms, $C_6H_7O_5(NO_2)_3$, and was consequently called trinitro-cellulose. The less nitrated product soluble in ether-alcohol was similarly supposed to be the dinitro-cellulose $C_6H_8O_5(NO_2)_2$. Later workers obtaining evidence of intermediate stages of nitration proposed to increase the formula of cellulose; Eder doubled it, Vieille quadrupled it, and Mendeleeff octupled it, giving 48 atoms of carbon to each molecule, and hydrogen and oxygen in proportion. A nitro-cellulose having the composition of the above-mentioned trinitro-compound would contain 14.14 percent nitrogen. Quite as much as this has never been found by the analysis of any product that has ever been obtained, but various investigators by nitrating with mixtures of nitric acid and phosphorous pentoxide, or with concentrated sulphuric and nitric acids and extracting the product with ether-alcohol have obtained percentages between 13.9 and 14.4. Lunge and Bebie found that with mixtures of sulphuric and nitric acids the highest percentage of nitrogen was attained, not with anhydrous acids, but with mixed acids containing 11 or 12 percent of water: with a mixture in which the proportions $H_2SO_4 : HNO_3 : H_2O$ : were 63.35 : 25.31 : 11.34 they produced a nitro-cotton containing 13.92 per cent N, but this was not stable. After keeping in the wet state it was reanalyzed and found to contain then only 13.5 percent N, and other nitro-cottons nitrated almost as highly were found to decompose rapidly until the same composition was reached, even though the material was kept under water. This corresponds very closely with the formula $C_{24}H_{29}O_{20}(NO_2)_{11}$, endeka-nitro-cellulose. Hence the authors conclude that the molecule with 24 atoms of carbon fits the facts sufficiently well, but point out that this is only the lower limit of the possible size of the cellulose molecule, as to the real magnitude of which there is little or no evidence.

(2) The following tabulation shows the percentage of nitrogen and the volume of NO gas evolved in the nitrometer by the several nitro-celluloses of the $C_{24}$ series (Die Explosivstoffe mit besondere berucksichtigung der Neuren Patente Bearbitet von, Dr. Richard Escales, Leipzig, von Veit, 1914):

| Parts nitrate | Designation | Formula | CC. No. per g. | Percent N. |
|---|---|---|---|---|
| 12 | Dodeka-nitro-cellulose | $C_{24}H_{28}O_8(NO_3)_{12}$ | 226. 27 | 14. 14 |
| 11 | Endeka-nitro-cellulose | $C_{24}H_{29}O_9(NO_3)_{11}$ | 215. 17 | 13. 47 |
| 10 | Deka-nitro-cellulose | $C_{24}H_{30}O_{10}(NO_3)_{10}$ | 203. 35 | 12. 75 |
| 9 | Ennea-nitro-cellulose | $C_{24}H_{31}O_{11}(NO_3)_9$ | 190. 75 | 11. 96 |
| 8 | Okto-nitro-cellulose | $C_{24}H_{32}O_{12}(NO_3)_8$ | 177. 19 | 11. 11 |
| 7 | Hepto-nitro-cellulose | $C_{24}H_{33}O_{13}(NO_3)_7$ | 162. 36 | 10. 18 |
| 6 | Hexa-nitro-cellulose | $C_{24}H_{34}O_{14}(NO_3)_6$ | 145. 96 | 9. 15 |
| 5 | Penta-nitro-cellulose | $C_{24}H_{35}O_{15}(NO_3)_5$ | 127. 91 | 8. 02 |
| 4 | Tetra-nitro-cellulose | $C_{24}H_{36}O_{16}(NO_3)_4$ | 107. 81 | 6. 76 |

(3) At the present time considerable doubt exists as to the exact structural formula for cellulose. Some of the recent investigations have indicated that the cellulose molecule may consist of extremely long chains having as many as 3,000 or more of the $(C_6H_{10}O_5)$ units in a single molecule. However, it is definitely known that nitrocellulose is not a true nitro body but is a nitric acid ester, or nitrate of cellulose; thus, the term nitrocellulose is a misnomer, but is standard through long usage. The same remarks apply to the terms "nitroglycerin" and "nitrostarch."

(4) In referring to the several forms of nitrocellulose, it is customary to speak of nitrocellulose with regard to its nitrogen content in percentage rather than to refer to it in respect to the number of $NO_3$ groups present in the molecule as is shown in the tabulation in (2) above. Paragraph 11 describes the purification procedure for pyro nitrocellulose, which when properly prepared contains 12.6 percent nitrogen $\pm 0.1$ percent, and paragraph 12, the manufacture of pyro powder from this material. It is important that careful control of the manufacturing process be exercised since it is necessary to produce a product uniform in solubility as well as in nitrogen content. If this uniformity is not obtained, difficulty is encountered in the subsequent manufacture of the pyro powder due to variations existing in the nitrocellulose. Some control over the viscosity and fineness of the pyrocotton is also desirable.

**11. Purification of pyrocotton.**—Under the general term of purification is included the following sequence of processes: preliminary boiling, pulping, poaching, screening, and wringing. It is impossible with the present limited knowledge of the cellulose molecule and of intermediate reactions occurring during nitration of the molecule to control the reaction to such an extent that a nitrocellulose consisting of but one nitro body will result from a certain reaction accomplished under a set of standard conditions. Products of the reaction always include certain nitrocelluloses of lower nitrogen content and other impurities. These bodies influence the stability of the whole mass and must therefore be removed before the desired stability of the pyrocotton can be obtained. The object, then, of the purification treatment is to insure a uniform stability by eliminating through hydrolysis or other means these unstable lower nitro bodies and other impurities. This is accomplished most easily by prolonged boiling in acid water which in the preliminary treatment has an acidity varying from 0.1 to 0.3 percent calculated as $H_2SO_4$.

*a. Boiling.*—The preliminary boiling process is carried out in large wooden tubs constructed preferably of cypress and having a false bottom. In the center of the tub is a square wooden duct resting on the false bottom. This duct serves as a heating chamber for the water by carrying a centrally located steam pipe. The water boils in this duct, rises to the top, flows over a false top, and is distributed through perforations onto the charge of pyrocotton. The actual boiling time must be 16 hours. The steam is then turned off, the excess water decanted, the tub refilled, and boiled again for 8 hours. This is repeated until each tub has had a 40-hour boil with

FIGURE 5.—Boiling tubs for purification of nitrocellulose before pulping, Picatinny Arsenal, N. J.

not less than four changes of water. Careful attention to details in the boiling tub house insures to the finished pyrocotton a more satisfactory stability than one in which these details have been disregarded.

*b. Pulping.*—The next process, pulping, has for its object reduction of the pyrocotton fibers to a finer state of division in order to remove the last traces of acidity occluded by the fibers. The pulping or beating operation is accomplished by machines similar to those used in the paper industry.

(1) The type of beater most generally used in manufacture of nitrocellulose is known as the Jordan engine. This machine consists of a series of broad-bladed knives set in a conical rotor, by means of which the nitrocellulose fibers, as they are forced through the machine along with a large volume of water, are reduced to the desired degree of fineness. The fineness of the material is indicated roughly when a handful squeezed free of excess water shows a clean break as it is broken in parts. The actual fineness is determined by laboratory test.

FIGURE 6.—General assembly of apparatus for pulping nitrocellulose showing concentrating sieve, Jordan engine and feed tank, Picatinny Arsenal, N. J.

(2) Another type of machine used for this purpose is the Miller duplex beater. The essential features of this pulping machine consist of a fixed set of knives at the bottom of a tube over which revolves a roller which is mounted in adjustable bearings and carries a removable set of knives. Pulping is accomplished by the rolls repeatedly drawing the pyrocotton between the two sets of knives and thus reducing the material to any desired degree of fineness. A weak sodium carbonate solution is used during this process for the purpose of neutralizing the acid retained within the fibers of the cotton and which is set free mechanically when these fibers are macerated. During

the first stage of the treatment a washer, consisting of a large octagonal box, covered with very fine wire screen, is lowered into the pulp to remove a part of the sour water, fresh water being added at the same time. The water thus removed passes to settling basins, where any pulp carried off mechanically is recovered. When the desired degree of fineness has been obtained, the material is ready for the next purifying process.

FIGURE 7.—Details of pulping equipment showing Jordan engine and feed tank, Picatinny Arsenal, N. J.

c. *Poaching.*—It has already been pointed out that in the pulping operation fibers of the pyrocotton are broken down mechanically so that the original physical texture of the cotton is destroyed. Preliminary boiling treatment reduced acidity of the fibers and of the interstitial material, but the pulping process by macerating these fibers set free an additional amount of acid. It is therefore necessary to repurify the pyrocotton by boiling. This operation is carried on in the poacher house in a manner somewhat similar to that described in the boiling tub house, but with the notable difference that the first boiling treatment is carried out in an alkaline solution. For this purpose there is dissolved 1 pound of sodium carbonate (soda ash) to a gallon of water, and for every 3,000 pounds of dry nitrocellulose there may be added 7.5 gallons of this solution. It is necessary to repeat the boiling operation five times, but the soda is only added during the first boiling. All the other treatments are made in a neutral solution.

FIGURE 8.—Poaching tubs for purification of pulped nitrocellulose, Picatinny Arsenal, N. J.

After the boiling treatments the pyrocotton is given at least 10 cold water washings. During all of these treatments a thorough agitation of the pyrocotton is essential so that it is necessary to employ mechanical stirrers driven by gears and shafting. At this stage of the operation it is necessary for the chemical laboratory to determine—

(1) Stability of the pyrocotton by K. I. test and heat test at 134.5° C.

(2) Percentage of nitrogen in the pyrocotton.

(3) Solubility of the pyrocotton in the ether-alcohol mixture.

(4) Degree of fineness.

(5) Ash.

Details of performing these tests are described in another chapter.

*d. Screening.*—After purifying the pyrocotton as described above, it is necessary to separate mechanically any foreign material or any portions of the product which may not have been properly macerated in the beater house. This is accomplished by means of the Packer screen. This piece of machinery consists of a large box, the bottom of which is fitted with a brass plate having slits 0.025 inch in width. The pulp is drawn through these slits by suction underneath the screen

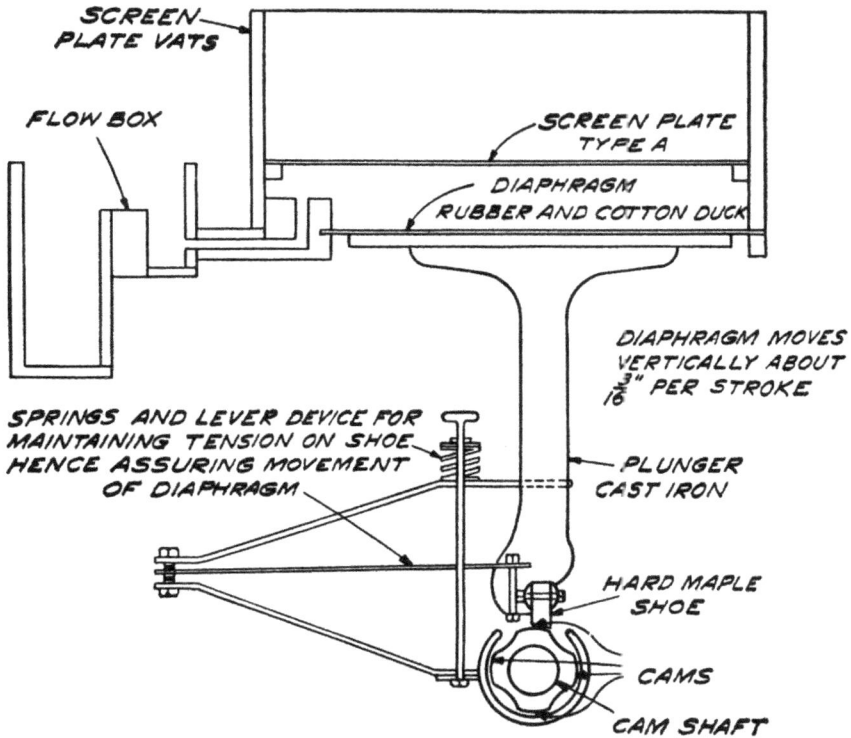

FIGURE 9.—Schematic sketch of Packer pulp screen.

and any particles which are too coarse to pass through are returned to the beater house for additional treatment. From the Packer screen the pulp is pumped into one of the large blending tubs where it is stored until needed in the next operation.

*e. Wringing.*—(1) *Purpose.*—Transference of the pyrocotton from the time of nitration up to this stage of manufacture is accomplished by having it suspended in water. It is the function of the wringers to remove water from the pulp so that the subsequent operation of dehydrating by means of alcohol will be done with minimum amount of water present. This wringing operation consists merely in forcing the water out of the pyrocotton by means of centrifugal action.

(2) *Wringer.*—The wringer consists of a perforated brass basket lined with a 24-mesh copper screen. This basket is connected by means of a shaft to a motor, which is so geared that the basket revolves at a speed of about 950 revolutions per minute. This centrifugal action forces the water out of the pyrocotton through the basket and so on down the drain pipe. The time of wringing is about 7 minutes. At the end of this operation another sample is sent to the laboratory for the purpose of determining amount of moisture remaining in the product. This moisture content averages between 26 and 28 percent.

If the wringers are operated at a uniform rate of speed for the same length of time moisture content will not vary more than 2 percent. This operation concludes the manufacture of pyrocotton.

**12. Formation of colloid.**—*a. Dehydration.*—(1) *Object.*—The pyro from the wringers containing approximately 28 percent moisture is transferred to storage and placed in warehouses to prevent freezing in wintertime until it is required for dehydration. The object of dehydration is to remove all water from the pyro and to add in its place the quantity of alcohol necessary to form the colloid with the ether which is added later. This amount varies within relatively small limits and is dependent upon the solubility of the pyro being used as shown by laboratory tests, and also to a certain extent upon size of granulation of the final powder. It is customary to add 1¼ pounds of alcohol for every pound dry weight of pyrocotton.

(2) *Operation.*—The dehydrating operation is conducted somewhat as follows: The press consists of a cylinder and movable piston operated by hydraulic pressure. The press is charged with pyrocotton and low pressure (about 250 pounds per square inch) is applied for a few moments, thus squeezing out a portion of the excess water. The predetermined amount of alcohol is then forced into the press by use of a pump, and the pressure increased to about 3,500 pounds per square inch. The alcohol functions first as an agent for displacing the water in the block and finally as a dehydrating agent. Its initial entrance into the block forces out a small portion of the remaining water; later however, it combines with the residual water and produces a block of pyro nearly free of water. The first portion of this alcohol contains relatively large amounts of water and is forced out of the press into the spent alcohol tank. The remaining amount, however, is about 90 percent alcohol. The spent alcohol resulting from this process is pumped

back into the storage tank and eventually rectified with addition of caustic soda to decompose dissolved or suspended nitrocellulose. It is then used again either in the dehydrating process or in the manufacture of ether.

(3) *Solvent required.*—The amount of solvent (ether-alcohol) necessary to form the colloid is determined from previous experience of manufacture. The general practice is to vary the amount of

FIGURE 10.—Details of dehydration press, Picatinny Arsenal, N. J.

solvent according to the web thickness of the powder; thus approximately 105 percent solvent is used in the manufacture of .30 caliber powder, 100 percent solvent for cannon powder whose web thickness is approximately 0.025 inch, and about 85 percent for powder having a web thickness of 0.185 inch. In the event that 100 percent of solvent is to be used, or 1 pound of solvent (1 part alcohol to 2 parts ether) for every pound of pyrocotton, it is necessary that the usual dehydrating press charge of 25 pounds dry weight of pyrocotton should produce a block weighing 33 pounds 4 ounces (25 pounds pyrocotton and 8 pounds 4 ounces alcohol).

   *b. Breaking of blocks.*—The dehydrated blocks must be first thoroughly broken up before the next operation of mixing is commenced. For this purpose they are transferred into a rotating drum or block breaker equipped on the inside with a wire screen and iron prongs. This barrel upon revolving throws the block against the prongs, thus breaking it into small lumps which lend themselves more readily to the mixing operation and which in turn insures a more even colloid.

   *c. Containers.*—From this point up to the time the powder is put into the solvent recovery (par. 14) the product is kept in closed containers as much as possible between the various steps in the manufacturing process in order to prevent excessive losses in solvent, which is an important point not only from the economical but also from the manufacturing standpoint, since excessive loss of solvent would entail difficulty or irregularity in subsequent screening and graining operations.

   *d. Mixing.*—(1) *Operation.*—The mixing operation is the next step in the formation of the colloid. As has been pointed out above, unless care is exercised during the dehydrating process in producing a block of uniform dehydration, it will be impossible to secure a good colloid. It is no less important that the ether be added to the

PA  M-8149

FIGURE 11.—Powder mixer tilted for discharging, Picatinny Arsenal, N. J.

mass in such a manner that the evaporating losses are minimized by incorporating the ether throughout the mass as quickly as possible. This is accomplished by use of a mixing machine. It consists of a covered water-cooled tank in which two shafts bearing curved agitator blades rotate in opposite directions, giving a kneading motion to the material in the mixer. During this agitation the ether is poured in rapidly in order to minimize loss of solvent by evaporation.

(2) *Stabilizer.*—It is also at this stage of the process that the so-called stabilizer is incorporated into the colloid. The material used for this purpose is diphenylamine, and there is dissolved in the ether enough of this substance so that the finished powder will contain between 0.90 and 1.10 percent diphenylamine. The object of adding diphenylamine at this stage is to incorporate it thoroughly throughout the colloid so that on long-continued storage any nitrous fumes which may be liberated within the powder will be absorbed by this so-called stabilizer. The many factors entering into the use of this material are more properly discussed in a later section on surveillance and stability.

*e. Pressing.*—(1) The colloid is next subjected in sequence to action of a preliminary blocking press, a macaroni press, and a final blocking press. Incorporation of ingredients as accomplished in mixing is really but a preparatory stage for final formation of colloid. this last step being completed by action of the presses.

(2) The preliminary blocking press consists merely of a cylinder and piston similar in action to the dehydrating press. It forms the colloid into a dense cylindrical mass by subjecting it to a compression of approximately 3,500 pounds per square inch. This so-called preliminary block is then transferred to the macaroni press. The operation here consists in straining the solid block of colloided matter through a heavy brass perforated plate on which are placed one 12-mesh steel plate, two sheets of 24 and one sheet of 36-mesh steel wire screens, at a pressure of 3,000 to 3,500 pounds per square inch, in such a manner that the material as it is ejected is similar in appearance and size to macaroni. As it leaves this press it falls by gravity into the cylinder of the final blocking press. This is similar in every respect to the preliminary blocking press and forms the colloid into final shape before it is taken to the graining press. The block is here subjected again to heavy pressure (approximately 3,500 pounds per square inch) for 1 to 2 minutes, thus completing the colloiding of the pyrocotton. The colloid now is entirely different in appearance from the material as drawn from the mixers for it has been changed from a mass resembling light brown sugar to a

dense, elastic, translucent brown or amber substance. These operations of pressing insure to the greatest possible degree a uniformly

FIGURE 12.—Preliminary blocking presses, Carney's Point, N. J.

thorough action of the solvent upon the pyro, and very nearly eliminate the possibility of having uncolloided nitrocotton in the finished powder.

**13. Graining and cutting.**—*a. Operation.*—The final operation from the standpoint of granulation of the powder occurs in the graining press room. These presses may be set either horizontally or vertically. Their action is to force the colloid through a steel die in such a manner that the expressed material which takes the form of a perforated or solid strand will be delivered at a uniform rate of speed under control of the operator at the press. The pressure which is necessary to force this colloid through the die is very great and is supplied by means of a hydraulic ram under a pressure of 2,500 to 3,800 pounds per square inch. The press head may be

FIGURE 13.—Macaroni and final blocking presses, Picatinny Arsenal, N. J.

equipped with one or more dies depending upon the capacity of the graining presses. When small-arms powder is being grained there may be 36 strands issuing simultaneously from the head. However, with a large caliber powder such as 16-inch gun it is customary to use but one die. The powder issues from the press head in the form of a flexible rope which is led over pulleys to a cutting machine. This cutting machine is capable of very fine adjustment and is so manipulated that the length of the grains may be closely controlled.

*b. Size of grain.*—Factors affecting size of the grain and its relation to the type of gun for which it is designed are discussed in section III.

14. **Solvent recovery.**—*a. Purpose.*—The powder as it comes from the cutter has a definite granular form and contains a considerable amount of the ether-alcohol solvent which must be removed. Hence, the powder is next subjected to a drying treatment for the purpose of removing the solvent from the powder grains. This drying process is of considerable importance in producing a uniform finished powder, and includes recovery of a large portion of the ether and alcohol solvent remaining in the powder. For this reason the initial

FIGURE 14.—Graining press room, Picatinny Arsenal, N. J.

process in drying powder is one of solvent recovery, although recovery of the solvent is only incidental in the powder manufacturing process.

*b. Equipment.*—There are three types of equipment that have been used successfully in recovery of solvent and initial drying of smokeless powder; first, the chamber type in which the powder is placed in a metal-lined box provided with a water sealed lid; second, the car type, which utilizes a solvent recovery car as a drying chamber, the car being loaded directly from the powder cutters; and third, the tank type in which the powder is transferred from the cutter room to a large metal tank.  In all of these types the operation of removing the solvent from the powder is the same.

  *c. Operation.*—(1) Warm air is circulated through the powder and is then forced over cold coils.  This change in temperature causes a precipitation of the solvent upon the coils and produces in effect a miniature fog.  The saturated air after passing over these cold coils loses its surplus solvent, is reheated, and then is again forced through the powder in a continuous cycle, in this manner completing the closed system of air circulation.  Length of treatment depends upon size of

FIGURE 15.—Graining press, Carney's Point, N. J.

the powder, the larger calibers requiring a greater length of time than the smaller ones.  As the solvent is removed from the powder the grains partially collapse or shrink and it is therefore necessary to control the rate at which the solvent is removed from the powder in order to produce a uniform finished product.  Furthermore, if the solvent is removed too rapidly the surface of the powder grains becomes dry and hard, this making more difficult the removal of the solvent from the interior of the grains.  Definite rules are laid down governing the length of time necessary for powder to remain in the solvent recovery building, these rules being the result of experiments and combining maximum efficiency with best results from the standpoint of drying.

(2) Temperature and times of heating in solvent recovery processes vary somewhat at different plants. A schedule which has been followed quite generally is outlined below.

(*a*) Propellant powders having web thickness up to 0.095 inch—
Raise to 30° and hold for 24 hours.
Raise to 38° and hold for 24 hours.
Raise to 45° and hold until total time of treatment has been 7 days.

FIGURE 16.—Charging floor, can type, solvent recovery house, Picatinny Arsenal, N. J.

(*b*) For powder of heavier web than 0.095 inch—
No heat for 48 hours.
Raise to 25° C. and hold for 24 hours.
Raise to 30° C. and hold for 24 hours.
Raise to 35° C. and hold for 24 hours.
Raise to 40° C. and hold for 24 hours.
Raise to 45° C. and hold until total time of drying of solvent recovery treatment has been 8 days.

FIGURE 17.—Can and discharge floor, can type, solvent recovery house, Picatinny Arsenal, N. J.

FIGURE 18.—Interior solvent recovery room, showing solvent recovery boxes, Picatinny Arsenal, N. J.

It is not practicable from an economic standpoint to reduce the solvent content of the powder to the desired degree in the solvent recovery treatment; hence, the final drying is accomplished as a separate operation.

*d. Ether recovery.*—Under normal operating conditions an appreciable portion of the ether in the solvent is lost due to exposure of the powder mass to the atmosphere unless means are provided for its recovery. In the more modern powder factories equipment is installed for recovery of the solvent vapors from the air.

**15. Drying.**—There are two separate types of drying operations, the first and most satisfactory, except from the standpoint of time, being the air-dry. The second method is known as the water-dry system and has a great advantage as to time saving.

*a. Air-dry treatment.*—(1) In this treatment the powder is transferred directly from the solvent recovery house to the dry house and placed in bulk in narrow bins. The time of drying varies with the granulation of the powder. For all granulations, however, there is a heating period of 30 days at 43° C. The temperature may then be raised to 55° C. The time required to drive off the volatile matter until the desired total volatile solvent content has been secured varies from about 30 days for the 75-mm powder to 90 or more days for 16-inch powder. In the case of powder having web thickness of more than 0.095 inch, a period of at least 2 weeks in the dry house without heating must precede any heating treatment.

(2) From time to time the laboratory analyzes a sample of the powder to determine if the required external moisture and volatile solvent contents have been reached. The desired external moisture content for air-dried powders varies inversely as the size of the grain from about 0.1 percent to 1.0 percent, while the total volatile content of the dried powders may vary from approximately 3.5 percent to 7.5 percent, depending upon the web thickness, the heavier web powders having the greater solvent contents. Control of moisture and volatile content of finished powders is of great importance since rate of burning and energy content of powder are reduced as the amount of solvent and moisture are increased.

*b. Water-dry treatment.*—The main difference between the air-dry process and the water-dry process is the difference in the surrounding medium. In the first case it is warm air and in the second warm water, but the object desired is the same in either case. Water is kept circulating throughout the powder at temperatures which vary by 10° increments from 25° to 55° C., for approximately 4 days for powders having a web thickness of approximately 0.020

inch. Later the powder is removed and air-dried for about 48 hours, this latter treatment requiring much less time to finish than when the powder has only the air-dry treatment. The external moisture content of water-dried powders may vary inversely with the size of powder from 0.9 percent to 1.4 percent.

*c. Continuous drier.*—A later development in the powder drying process is the so-called continuous drier. This differs from the ordinary dry house treatment in that drying the powder is accomplished in between 4 and 5 hours, depending upon size of granulation. The powder enters the dry house from the water-dry system, is hoisted

FIGURE 19.—Interior water-dry house, Picatinny Arsenal, N. J.

to a hopper and then slides by gravity into a shaking screen. This screen removes foreign material and drops the powder to a bucket conveyor of the ordinary type. The powder is then hoisted to the top of the building where it is thrown into a drying chute. This chute is approximately 6 inches in thickness, 5 feet in width, and about 10 feet in length, and is equipped with baffles running crosswise in the direction of its smallest dimensions. A series of screens on the side wall provides the means for the passage of warm air through the powder; and a temperature of 50° C. is maintained by this means at the bottom of the chute. A shaking device near the floor is capable of such regulation that the rate of discharge from the drier and consequently the volatile content of the powder is controlled by the speed at which this shaker is operated and by the amount of clearance between the shaker and the bottom of the chute. In one of the largest war plants one continuous drier was capable of drying to correct moisture and volatile content 100,000 pounds of 75-mm powder in 24 hours.

**16. Blending.**—*a. Powder lots.*—The next step and an important one from the standpoint of uniformity of firing is the proper mixing or blending of a certain arbitrary amount of powder. For the larger caliber guns it is customary to blend or mix a complete lot of 100,000 pounds of powder, but for the smaller caliber powders, particularly for the small-arms powders, lots ranging from 15,000 to 50,000 pounds are more usual.

FIGURE 20.—Cannon powder blender, Picatinny Arsenal, N. J.

*b. Operation and equipment.*—(1) The blending operation consists merely in transference of powder by means of gravity from one bin to another, this transference resulting in thorough mixing of all the lot. These bins are so constructed that when full of a lot of powder the powder assumes the shape of a double cone with one apex pointed down toward the discharge pipe and the other apex pointed up toward the top of the bin. The proper construction of these bins from the standpoint of the correctness of angles at the sides of the bin is very important. If the sides of the bin are too steep, the powder will slide down toward the apex of the lower cone. If, on the other hand, the sides are built on too gradual a slope the powder will not flow freely from the bin and it would be necessary to use a raking device in order to empty the bin toward the end of the lot. It is essential therefore that a point midway between these two be found, a point so selected that the powder will not slide down the side of the bin, yet at the same time will insure a complete emptying and mixing of the lot. These angles have been determined and when the principles are observed no difficulty results from lack of proper blending. After two or three cycles from one bin to the other have been completed, the powder is weighed and boxed.

(2) Another type of blender was formerly used at Picatinny Arsenal. In the place of two bins set one upon the other as in the old type—an awkward arrangement which necessitated a building at least 100 feet high—two separate buildings were constructed about 100 feet apart. The bottom of one bin was connected with the top of the other by an endless belt. There were then two belts operated independently of each other for transference of the powder from the bottom of one bin to the top of the other. The arrangement at the bottom of each bin was such that the powder might be boxed in either building. When it was desired to empty one bin and transfer to the other for the purpose of blending, it was necessary only to put the belt in motion and open the chute. The speed of the belt was such that 100,000 pounds were hoisted in about 75 minutes, a speed not possible with the older type of blender. The powder was charged into a hopper at the base of one tower from bags if coming from the dry house, or from boxes if the powder was being reblended, on to a conveyer belt, carried to the top of the second tower, and dropped into the bin until the entire lot had been transferred to this bin. The conveyer belt at the base of this second tower was then started, the powder carried to the top of the first tower, and thence into the bin, thus completing the cycle. The blending comprised four complete cycles.

*c. Storage container.*—After the blending is completed the lot of powder is boxed and stored. The powder container used for storage is merely an airtight zinc box about which is built a wooden box completely covering and protecting the metal inside. It is of such a size as to hold from 110 to 140 pounds of smokeless powder, depending upon type of box. These boxes are tested for air leaks to insure the powder retaining the same moisture and volatile content as when withdrawn from the dry house. In recent years an all-metal box has been used for the larger caliber powders.

**17. FNH and NH powders for cannon.**—*a. Development.*—At the outbreak of the World War in 1914, the United States Army and Navy employed the same type of straight nitrocellulose powder, the manufacture of which has been described above. After the experiences in the war certain weaknesses in the standard propellent powder were recognized:

(1) *Hygroscopicity.*—The standard nitrocellulose type of powder if exposed to the atmosphere is subject to change. The volatile solvent,

FIGURE 21.—Powder weighing and packing room, Picatinny Arsenal, N. J.

ether-alcohol, used in manufacture is not completely removed, the powder retaining from 3 to 7.5 percent, depending upon size of grain. In a warm, dry atmosphere this residual solvent partially escapes and the rate of burning of the powder is increased. On the other hand, if the powder is exposed to a humid atmosphere, it absorbs moisture and the rate of burning is decreased. Thus, ballistic properties of the powder are appreciably affected by changes in atmospheric conditions to which the powder may be exposed.

(2) *Flash.*—Another objection to the pyropowder was the fact that when fired it produces a large, brilliant flash at the muzzle of the gun.

This proved to be a serious objection during the World War owing to the great amount of night firing conducted, since the flash aided the enemy in locating positions of the guns.

The need was recognized for a nonvolatile, nonhygroscopic, and flashless powder which would still retain the property of being substantially smokeless. Such powder has been developed since the World War, and is designated FNH if flashless, or NH if used in weapons in which flashlessness is not attained.

FIGURE 22.—Final air testing of powder boxes, Picatinny Arsenal, N. J.

b. *FNH powder.*—(1) The FNH type of powder has been obtained by adding to the nitrocellulose inert or partially inert materials for the purpose of cooling the products of combustion and reducing the hygroscopicity of the powder. Such a powder may be flashless in certain weapons but not flashless in others, since flashlessness is dependent not only upon composition of the powder, but upon relationship between quantity of powder used as a charge and length of bore of the weapon, weight of projectile, etc. While it might appear possible to obtain flashlessness in any weapon by merely increasing the amount of flash-reducing agent in the powder composition, such a procedure may be impracticable either because of increased smoke produced or reduction in potential of the powder. While the present type of FNH powder has a lower potential than the standard pyrocellulose powder, it has sufficient potential to permit its use in all weapons without change in ballistic requirements.

(2) The manufacture of the FNH powder can be carried out in the same equipment and plant used for manufacture of the standard pyrocellulose powder. However, details of the processes for the two types of powder differ in many respects.

Section III

GRANULATION OF SMOKELESS POWDER

Paragraph
General_____ 18
Form and size of grains_____ 19
Control of grain dimensions in powder manufacture_____ 20

**18. General.**—The propellent powder used as a charge for the gun possesses a certain force or latent power which upon combustion becomes a kinetic or moving force which drives the projectile from the muzzle of the gun. When powder is ignited it undergoes chemical decomposition and is converted by change of state, that is, from solid to gas, into a volume greater than that originally occupied by the powder. Simultaneously with this change of state, the heat generated by the explosion expands the volume of gas produced and increases its pressure, and finally sets the projectile in motion.

Rapid development of gas pressure within the gun should be of such a progressive nature that the force exerted does not attain its maximum at time of ignition (as would be the case if a high explosive in its usual form were used as a propellant), but rather attains it by a relatively gradual rise. Control of this pressure lies in the composition of the powder, form or shape of individual powder grains, and size or dimension of any particular form of grain. Granulation determines the area of the burning surface of the grain which in turn controls rate of combustion, and through that, the pressure.

A brief consideration of factors influencing and determining proper granulation of powder will involve discussion first, of the best form of powder grains and second, factors which determine size of grains.

**19. Form and size of grains.**—*a. Form.*—(1) *Ballistic requirements.*—The best form of granulation from a ballistic point of view is first, that which with the smallest weight of charge will impart to the projectile the prescribed muzzle velocity within the permitted limit of maximum pressure; second, that which will cause minimum erosion to the bore; and third, that which shows maximum regularity in ballistics.

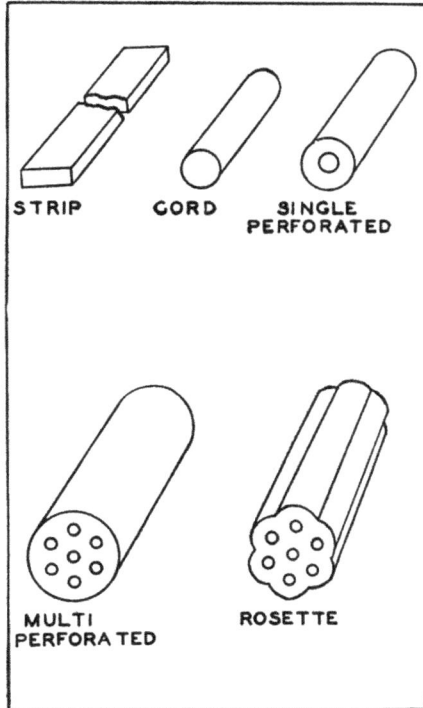

FIGURE 23.—Forms of powder grains.

The grains burn uniformly from the surface and the rate of burning varies directly with the pressure; the greater the burning surface, the

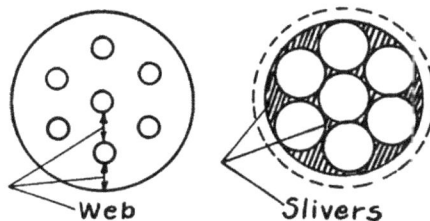

FIGURE 24.—Cross section of multiperforated powder grains.

higher the pressure, other things being equal. The shape of the grain is a direct factor in determining the total amount of burning surface of a given weight of powder.

(2) *Types.*—Smokeless powders are granulated in regular geometrical forms of various sizes and lengths. The principal forms in use are the solid cord, the flat strip, the single perforated cylinder, and the multiperforated cylinder shown in Figure 23. The most important dimension of these grains is the "web" thickness or minimum thickness between any two parallel surfaces.

(3) *Burning action.*—(*a*) Since smokeless powder of any grain form burns only on the surface and in parallel layers perpendicular to the surface, it is readily apparent that the extent of change of surface of the powder grains as they are consumed varies widely among the different grain forms. Thus, grains in form of cords or strips burn with a continually decreasing surface until the grains are entirely consumed, whereas the multiperforated grain burns with a continually increasing surface until it is nearly consumed; although the exterior surface of the multiperforated grain decreases in area during burning, the interior surfaces formed by the perforations increase during burning so that the net result is an increase in burning area until the grains are largely consumed. Any form of grain which presents a decreasing surface area during combustion is termed a degressive burning grain, while all forms which present an increasing surface as combustion progresses are styled progressive burning grains. Since tubular or single perforated grains show only slight change of surface during combustion, they are usually referred to as neutral grains.

(*b*) Figure 24 shows that when the inner and outer webs of the multiperforated grain have burned through, pieces of triangular cross section called slivers remain unburned. When 7 perforations are present, 12 of these slivers are produced, these constituting about 15 percent of the total weight of the grain. These slivers burn degressively and are usually consumed in the bore of the weapon but if this is relatively short or if a reduced charge is fired and thus relatively low pressure is developed, the slivers may be expelled unburned from the muzzle. The form of grain known as the Walsh or rosette grain, (fig. 23) having the usual 7 perforations but with the outer periphery of the grain scalloped, has been used in some seacoast mortars. This type of grain reduces amount of slivers and therefore reduces or eliminates amount of unburned powder ejected from the weapon.

(4) *Use.*—(*a*) *Multiperforated.*—The United States Army and Navy have favored the use of the multiperforated grain form since its small initial burning surface per unit weight of powder results in a slower rise of pressure during initial stages of combustion. This slower rise of pressure allows maximum pressure to be developed at a point farther from the breech than is obtained with the degressive

type of grains. Our guns are designed to withstand a pressure increasing to the maximum at a point in the bore just ahead of the powder chamber. With the maximum pressure at this point, a higher pressure is exerted on the projectile throughout its travel to the muzzle than would be the case if the peak pressure occurred in the powder chamber.

(*b*) *Single perforated.*—Single perforated powders are used for United States small arms, minor caliber cannon, and for certain howitzers largely because of the difficulty in extruding a multiperforated powder when exceptionally thin webs are required to meet ballistic requirements.

*b. Size.*—(1) *Weapon factors.*—In general, for any given grain form the size of grain to be produced depends on the type of weapon in which it is to be used. It is generally true that the web thickness of powder must increase with the caliber or power of the weapon. The ratio of web thickness to caliber is not the same, however, for the different classes or types of artillery weapons, namely, guns, howitzers, and mortars. This is due to the marked difference in the ratio of the length of the tubes to the caliber of the tubes among the various weapons.

(*a*) *Length.*—In comparing the three types of weapons as to length, the gun is the longest, its length ranging from 40 to 60 times the bore of the gun (calibers); howitzers are medium in length, and mortars the shortest. Therefore, the mortar type would require a powder with a larger burning surface and hence smaller granulation than either a gun or a howitzer of the same caliber, However, the gun as a class gives the highest degree of accuracy, permits the longest travel of the projectile, and imparts the highest muzzle velocity. The seacoast mortars are short guns and in firing them there is always a large amount of unburned powder slivers thrown from the muzzle, except when the sliverless or Walsh grain is used. This grain, as has been pointed out before, by providing a larger burning surface burns more quickly and thus practically eliminates this undesirable feature.

(*b*) *Caliber.*—The calibers of seacoast weapons range from 3 to 16 inches and are permanently mounted in fortifications. Field weapons, or mobile artillery, are designed to accompany or follow an army in the field, and are smaller in caliber except in some of the railroad mounts. Depending upon the type of weapon, however, granulation of the powder must be so controlled that the functions of the different weapons are best served. Howitzers are used only in mobile artillery. "For each caliber of gun there is designed a corresponding howitzer of an equal degree of mobility, and the caliber of each howitzer is the same as that of the gun of the next lower degree of mobility; that is, the howitzer corresponding in mobility to one of the guns is of the same caliber as the next heavier gun and uses the same projectile." (Tschappat.) (See par. 89.)

(c) *Powder chamber capacity.*—Since each type of gun has its specified size of powder chamber, it is necessary to ascertain this capacity before designing the granulation of the powder. Other factors being equal, the greater the capacity of the powder chamber, the greater the size of the powder grains. For instance, the capacity of the powder chamber for the 12-inch mortar, M1890, is 2,674 cubic inches, and 12-inch mortar, M1912, 3,770 cubic inches, using the same weight projectile (700 pounds). The "average web" for M1890 is 0.0600 inch and for M1912, 0.0760 inch.

(2) *Web.*—The term "web" referred to in (1)(c) above is the measure of powder grain size most commonly considered in design work. It is defined as the least burning thickness from the edge of one surface to the edge of the next surface in the diametric direction. The "average web" is the mean of "inner" and "outer" webs (multiperforated grains). Relatively slight adjustments in the average web of a powder result in appreciable changes in required weight of charge and resultant maximum pressure (velocity remaining constant).

(3) *Final dimension factors.*—In establishing size of powder grains for a particular weapon, the principal features which affect final dimensions of the grains are weight of the projectile, prescribed velocity, weight of charge, and percentage of moisture and volatiles allowed to remain in the powder.

(a) *Effect of projectile weight and prescribed velocity.*—In general, the heavier the projectile or the higher the prescribed velocity, the larger the powder grains required, holding the maximum pressure within the proper limit. "An increased weight of projectile will result in an increased maximum pressure in the gun if the same muzzle velocity is to be maintained with the same powder, size of powder chamber, and length of travel. The maximum pressure for any gun being fixed, the use of a heavier projectile will usually require the use of a slower powder, and if the increase in weight is very great it will require an increase in the size of the powder chamber, or in the length of the gun, or in both dimensions." (Tschappat, p. 518.)

(b) *Relation between weight of charge and grain dimensions.*—By varying the web thickness of the powder for any given weapon and projectile, it is possible to alter appreciably the weight of propelling charge to meet ballistic requirements. For example, pyro powders have been accepted for use with the 12.7-pound projectile in the 3-inch antiaircraft gun, with weights of charge varying from 4.88 to 5.66 pounds. This variation in weight of charge resulted from variation in the web thickness of the lots which ranged from .0339 inch to .0444 inch. The pressure of course was higher for the powder of lower web, being 34,000 pounds per square inch as compared to 28,700 pounds per square inch for the heavier web.

From an economic standpoint it is obviously desirable to maintain the weight of charge as low as practicable, and hence from this standpoint as thin a web should be used as is compatible with pressure requirements.

In the case of zone charges especially, it is desirable to granulate the powder with as thin a web as practicable so that higher pressures will be obtained in firing the inner zones. Better velocity uniformity is commonly obtained at the higher pressures.

(c) *Effect of moisture and volatiles.*—After graining, the bulk of the solvent is dried out, but 2 percent to 8.5 percent may remain in pyro powder as moisture and volatiles or total volatiles, the amount depending upon size of the grain. No better description of the effect of moisture and volatiles can be given than the following from Tschappat, page 115:[1]

The alcohol used in the solvent contains 5 percent water, which generally remains in the powder after drying. Additional water may be absorbed from the air during the process of manufacturing and handling. Recent lots of powder also contain approximately 1 percent of a stabilizer, and .30 caliber rifle powders contain, in addition, a small percentage of graphite.

Smokeless pyro powder may, therefore, be considered to be a mixture of nitrocellulose, alcohol, water, and sometimes a stabilizer and graphite. Most of the ether used is evaporated out during the drying process.

From calculations it is found that the energy per pound of pure nitrocellulose of 12.60 percent nitrogen is about 1,425,000 foot-pounds per pound. If now, an inert material, that is, one that takes no part in the reaction at combustion, is mixed with the nitrocellulose, the energy per pound of the resulting material will be less than that of pure nitrocellulose. For instance, if 0.99 pounds of pure nitrocellulose of 12.60 percent N is mixed with 0.01 pound of inert material, the inert material will be 1 percent of the total weight and the energy per pound of the resulting material will evidently be $1,425,000 \times 0.99 = 1,410,750$ foot-pounds per pound.

Now, of the materials entering powder as given above, water is considered as having the same effect as the same percentage of inert matter. Alcohol has

---

[1] Data slightly revised to bring up to date.

a greater effect than inert matter for the reason that the carbon contained in it combines with the $CO_2$, resulting from the combustion of the nitrocellulose, thus forming a larger quantity of CO and a smaller quantity of $CO_2$, than in the combustion of pure nitrocellulose. Theoretical considerations and practical tests indicate that the effect of 1 percent alcohol in reducing the energy per pound of nitrocellulose is equal to the effect of 2.5 percent inert matter.

In the same way the effect of 1 percent stabilizer, which is higher in carbon content than alcohol, is shown to be equal to the effect of 4 percent inert matter. Graphite, though entirely carbon, does not readily take part in the reaction and, therefore, the effect of 1 percent graphite in reducing the energy per pound of nitrocellulose is considered equal to that of 2.5 percent inert matter.

Consequently, the granulation of the powder must be so calculated that it will counteract the reduction of the energy of the powder by the solvent remaining after drying. In order to give more energy, the burning surface should be increased by diminishing the average web measurements or the size of the grain, or by changing the form of the grain.

**20. Control of grain dimensions in powder manufacture.—** *a. Specification requirements.—*U. S. Army Specifications for cannon powder contain the following general requirements regarding dimensions of powder grains, such requirements being established to control bulk density of the powder as well as burning characteristics:

(1) *Multiperforated grains.—*(*a*) Average grain length (**L**) shall be from 2.10 to 2.50 times average grain diameter (D).

(*b*) Average grain diameter (D) shall be approximately 10 times average diameter of perforations (d).

(*c*) Difference between average outer web thickness ($W_o$) and average inner web thickness ($W_i$) shall not exceed 15 percent of the web thickness ($W_a$).

(2) *Single perforated grains.—*(*a*) Average grain length (L) shall be from 3 to 6 times average diameter (D).

(*b*) Average grain diameter (D) shall be approximately 3 times average diameter of perforation (d).

*b. Dies.—*(1) *Description.—*Figure 25 shows the general design of die through which the multiperforated powder is extruded from the graining presses during manufacture. As the powder comes from the graining press it contains from 40 percent to 50 percent solvent and is called "green" because the solvent has not been extracted by the drying processes. The green powder has about the same dimensions as the steel die through which it has just been pressed. The die body A consists of a steel block designed to hold the pin plate B, the water jacket C (having an inlet and outlet for water used for cooling the die while running the powder) and a closing screw D for the water jacket. The pin plate consists of a perforated plate to which are attached wires or pins E, which form the perforations in the grain, and the plug F, which holds the pins in place when the die is not in use. The dimensions for both the die body and pin plate are called die dimensions.

(2) *Dimension determination.*—(*a*) *General factors.*—It is necessary to calculate the dimensions of the die very accurately, as there are many factors which cause the measurements of the green powder to differ from those of the die. Among these factors is the spring of the pins (or needle wire) by which action the pins are drawn together as the powder is being pressed through the die, and which has the effect of decreasing the inner web. Another factor is the consistency of the powder as it is being grained. The softer the powder, the more it will contract as it goes through the die, thus causing the green dimensions to be less than the die dimensions.

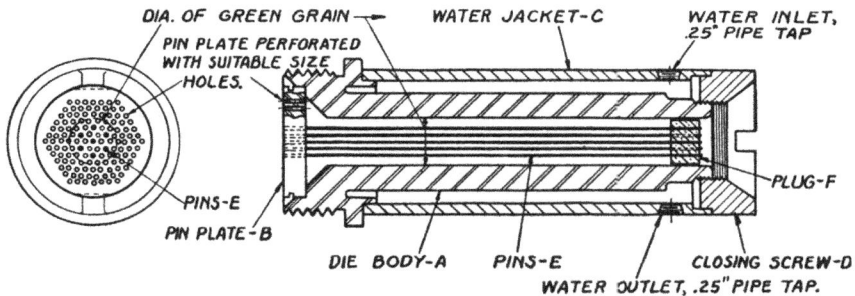

FIGURE 25.—Powder die assembly used for cylindrical grains.

(*b*) *Powder shrinkage.*—In order to determine the size of die required to manufacture a powder of given dry web, it is necessary to know the extent to which the powder will contract or shrink after the solvent has been removed. The shrinkage is expressed as the percentage reduction of a given dimension such as the web (W) from the green to the dry form. The percentage shrinkage for the various dimensions varies considerably; for example, the shrinkage in length of grain may be as small as 5 percent, while the web shrinkage may vary from 25 to 35 percent. The shrinkage for the inner web (W₁) for multiperforated powders is usually less than the shrinkage for the outer web (Wₒ); furthermore, the percent shrinkage will vary considerably with composition, quantity of solvent, physical characteristics of the nitrocellulose, and size of grain. The shrinkage which occurs when the various grain sizes are manufactured according to a standardized procedure is determined by the actual manufacture of small experimental lots of the approximate grain sizes involved.

Once the dry dimensions are decided upon and the percent shrinkage known for a given composition and manufacturing procedure, the powder can be made with a reasonable assurance that it will dry closely to the size expected.

(*c*) *Method.*—The following problem and calculations illustrate the method used for the determination of die dimensions to manu-

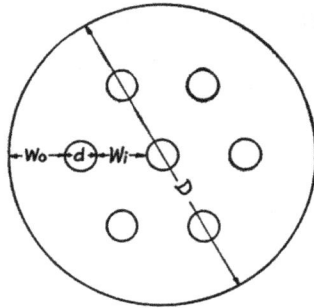

CYLINDRICAL GRAINS 7 PERFORATIONS
DRY DIMENSIONS (APPROX.)
$D = 10 d$
$W_o = W_i + 5\% W_i$
$W_a = \dfrac{W_o + W_i}{2}$
$D$ = OUTSIDE DIAMETER
$d$ = DIAMETER OF PERFORATION
$W_o$ = OUTER WEB
$W_i$ = INNER WEB

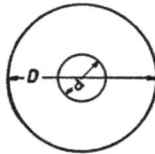

CYLINDRICAL GRAIN SINGLE PERFORATION
DRY DIMENSION, $D = 3 d$
$D$ = OUTSIDE DIAMETER
$d$ = DIAMETER OF PERFORATION

FIGURE 26.—Grain perforations.

facture a powder of any given dry dimensions. The symbols used in these calculations are described in figure 26. When the symbol refers to a green dimension, it is followed by the letter "g" and when it refers to the dry powder dimension, it is followed by the letter "d."

*Problem.*—A die is desired for the manufacture of a powder of the multiperforated grain form to have an average dry web ($W_{ad}$) of 0.0220 inch and a dry perforation diameter ($d_d$) of 0.0127 inch. The shrinkages for this composition are perforation, 21.0 percent; outer web, 35.0 percent; inner web, 25 percent.

*Solution.*—Pin size $(dg) = 0.0127 \div (100-21) \times 100 = 0.01606$ inch.

It is considered desirable to manufacture powders with outer web $(W_{od})$ slightly larger, usually about 5 percent, than the inner web $(W_{id})$; therefore, the outer web will be 2.5 percent greater than the average web or 0.02255 inch, while the inner web will be 2.5 percent less than the average web or 0.02155 inch.

Since it is apparent from figure 26 that the bore diameter of the die, which is equal to the diameter of the green grain $(Dg)$, is the sum of the thickness of the green inner and outer webs plus the diameter of the green perforations, it is necessary to determine the green dimensions of the inner and outer webs. The green outer web

PA   M-8524

FIGURE 27.—Die body, pin plate, water jacket, and smokeless powder grains for 155-mm gun.

$(W_{og})$ is calculated as follows: $0.02255 \div (100-35) \times 100 = 0.0357$ inch. The green inner web $(W_{ig})$ then is calculated similarly as 0.0287 inch. With the above data, the bore diameter $(D_g)$ becomes $3(0.01606) + 2(0.0287) + 2(0.0347)$, or 0.17498 inch.

It is now necessary to calculate the diameter of the circle on which the centers of the pins must be set in the pin plate. This dimension is referred to as pin circle diameter and is equal to $2(W_{ig}) + 2(dg)$ which in this case is 0.0895 inch.

There remains yet the length of grain or the cut to be determined. Since the shrinkage in length is small and since the ratio of length of grain to diameter may vary from 2.10 to 2.5, the green diameter $(D_g)$ may be multiplied by 2.5 to obtain the length of cut. If a closer controlled length of cut is desired, the shrinkage in length must be known and the green length calculated accordingly.

SECTION IV

# STABILITY AND STORAGE OF SMOKELESS POWDER

|  | Paragraph |
|---|---|
| General | 21 |
| Stability tests | 22 |
| Causes of instability | 23 |
| Stabilizers | 24 |
| Storage | 25 |
| Shipment | 26 |

**21. General.**—The subject of stability of smokeless powder involves both safety in storage and uniformity in ballistics. In the discussion upon the purification of nitrocellulose it was pointed out that the processes of boiling are made necessary from the fact that a pure product, or more properly one definite nitrate, cannot be prepared. Present knowledge of the cellulose molecule and of intermediate reactions occurring during nitration of the molecule limits any attempt at preparation of a single nitrate, and while complete hydrolysis of lower nitrates is sought in the boiling processes, there is no assurance that this reaction is the only one concerned, nor is it proven that there are not other factors influencing speed and completeness of the reaction. In spite of the elaborate process of purification followed out to insure stability of the finished powder, this program is extended by incorporating in the colloid 1 percent dry weight of diphenylamine.

**22. Stability tests.**—The nitrocellulose for use in making powder is said to be stable or is said to have good stability when it passes the KI test and the heat test at 134.5° C., while the stability of the finished powder is determined by means of the heat test at 134.5° C., and the test in the surveillance chamber, which is maintained at a temperature of 65.5° C.

There is no test, however, of the stability of smokeless powder which is infallible, or which indicates in more than a general way the safety of the powder from the storage standpoint. The idiosyncrasies and the unreliability of the KI test are too well known to require more than passing mention. The heat test at 134.5° C. serves as a criterion for the incomplete hydrolysis of the lower nitrates and for the presence of sulphuric esters (cellulose sulphates). Such impurities are capable of giving a low test for "salmon pink," or an early explosion in this test. The surveillance tests of smokeless powder are not entirely satisfactory from the standpoint of uniformity of results and also from the standpoint of elapsed time necessary to obtain any data.

The principal weakness of the above tests, however, is that they involve the use of only small samples which may not be truly representative of the large quantity of powder comprising a lot. Since a powder lot is commonly a blend of portions which may not be in precisely the same condition as regards stability, it is often uncertain whether variations in the results of stability tests are due to the test methods or to actual variations in the condition of the powder comprising the lot.

**23. Causes of instability.**—All organic compounds can be decomposed by heat. Explosives in general are chemical compounds which undergo decomposition when subjected to only moderately elevated temperatures, most of them being unable to withstand prolonged exposure to a temperature as high as 200° C. The resistance of such compounds to decomposition by heat is an inherent property dependent upon the structure of the molecule as is color, melting point, odor, etc.

Nitrocellulose is one of the least resistant explosives to heat that is used in military ammunition. Since nitrocellulose is the essential constituent of smokeless powder, the stability of the latter is determined largely by the nitrocellulose, and the powder consequently has relatively low resistance to heat. Decomposition of smokeless powder is so rapid above 200° C. that spontaneous ignition will occur within a few minutes. The rate of decomposition is reduced as the temperature is lowered until at atmospheric temperatures only very slight decomposition will occur over a period of many years, provided the powder is not subjected to influences other than temperature which tend to promote its decomposition.

Any chemical compound can be decomposed by reaction with certain other compounds. The reactivity of compounds is also an inherent property depending upon the structure of the molecules. Nitrocellulose, being an organic ester, possesses the characteristics of esters in general and can be decomposed by boiling water, such decomposition being promoted if acids or alkalies are present. The reactivity of nitrocellulose with water, acids, and alkalies is of special importance because of the use of these compounds in the process of manufacture. It is essential that they be thoroughly removed before the nitrocellulose is manufactured into powder; otherwise, the normal rate of decomposition produced by temperature effects will be increased by reaction of the material with the impurities remaining in the nitrocellulose.

In the nitration of cellulose, the nitrating mixture of nitric and sulphuric acid acts on the impurities contained in the cellulose as well as on the cellulose itself. Thus, cellulose sulphate and sulphates or nitrates of oxycellulose, hydrocellulose, and other cellulose complexes may be formed as impurities in the nitrocellulose. Such impurities are also decomposed by heat and some of them are indicated to be more readily affected than nitrocellulose. Hence, their presence tends to reduce the stability of the nitrocellulose and of powders made from it.

From the above discussion it is evident that to obtain nitrocellulose of maximum stability, great care must be exercised to eliminate impurities which are formed in the nitration process and also any acid or alkali which is present during the purification treatment. In order that powder made from such nitrocellulose will exhibit the maximum degree of stability under any temperature conditions in storage, it is necessary that the powder be protected from reaction with moisture or other materials which react with nitrocellulose.

**24. Stabilizers.**—Prior to 1908 little was done from the manufacturing standpoint to standardize methods of purification then in practice. In fact, the importance of the whole subject of stability of explosives was not recognized to the same extent as at present and consequently had not received the same consideration. In mixing the colloid it was the practice to incorporate a small amount of an organic dye which served the purpose of an indicator rather than a stabilizer.

The indicator which found the widest application was rosaniline, and its adoption was due to the fact that upon development of any marked acidity produced from decomposition of the smokeless powder, the red color of the dye in the powder grains faded to a yellow, which fact served to indicate instability.

Use of diphenylamine was not general until the latter part of 1908, and its function was different from that of rosaniline, for it has the property of combining with free $NO_2$. Upon development of the free oxides of nitrogen in smokeless powder, the diphenylamine undergoes progressive nitration (Buisson, p. 1172) (see par. 89), as indicated in the following series of reactions:

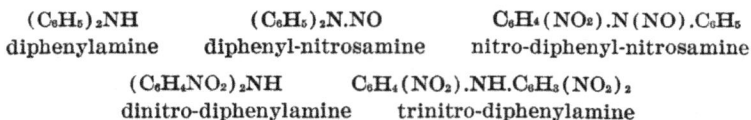

$(C_6H_5)_2NH$      $(C_6H_5)_2N.NO$      $C_6H_4(NO_2).N(NO).C_6H_5$
diphenylamine      diphenyl-nitrosamine      nitro-diphenyl-nitrosamine

$(C_6H_4NO_2)_2NH$      $C_6H_4(NO_2).NH.C_6H_3(NO_2)_2$
dinitro-diphenylamine      trinitro-diphenylamine

These separate substances may be detected by various quantitative and qualitative reactions, and it was formerly thought that when any of the tests applied to the powder were positive, they indicated an impaired stability. However, more recent work has indicated that nitrosodiphenylamine itself is an excellent stabilizer so that the presence of nitrosodiphenylamine does not necessarily indicate impaired stability.

**25. Storage.**—It has already been pointed out that moisture and volatile content of smokeless powder are important factors in determining weight of charge and pressure to be expected for required muzzle velocity. In order that this percentage will remain constant it is necessary that the powder be stored in airtight containers so constructed that they may be easily filled, tested, piled, and emptied. With small-arms powder it is customary to line the inside of the container with a muslin bag, the object being to keep the powder entirely free from dust, chips, or other extraneous material.

*a. Containers.*—(1) *Description.*—(*a*) The powder container consists of a wooden box, zinc-lined, about 26 by 16 by 11 inches. There are two types, the so-called export type, having a capacity of 140 pounds, and the other, the Picatinny Arsenal type, having a capacity of 110 pounds. The cover is provided with an outside ring, locking ring, and rubber gasket, assembled in such a way that when a lever is forced down on the top of the box, tension is put upon the lug in such a manner that there is no possibility of air leaks. Each box is tested before being filled by having a small hole drilled in the cover, applying compressed air, and noting the reading on the pressure gage attached to the air line.

(*b*) In recent years a steel container has been standardized for storage of the larger granulation of cannon powder. These have the advantage of more substantial construction and, hence, less expense for inspection and repair to guard against air leaks.

(2) *Testing.*—In order to detect the presence of deteriorated powder and remove it from storage before spontaneous combustion can occur, each box in storage over 5 years old is tested by inserting a strip of tenth-normal methyl violet paper above the powder. This paper is examined and replaced by a fresh strip each year. The contents of any box in which the test strip becomes bleached in 12 months or less is considered hazardous for continued storage and is removed and disposed of. Since this test was instituted not one single fire due to deteriorated powder has occurred.

(3) *Piling.*—In piling, the boxes are placed on their narrow sides at an angle of about 20°, so as to permit removal of the lids and insertion of the methyl violet test papers without removing considerable powder from the boxes. They should not be piled closely together for the reason that such a procedure defeats proper ventilation. The boxes are commonly piled 6 high, this being about all the usual magazine space permits.

*b. Magazines.*—(1) *Temperature.*—Magazines for storage of smokeless powder should be kept dry, and should be so situated that there is a minimum variation in temperature. This latter point is an important one from the standpoint of maintaining standard moisture and volatile content. In those instances where a wide range in temperature obtains there is always the added risk of the powder containers tending to develop leaks, due to the difference in the atmospheric pressure inside and outside the zinc boxes. The most satisfactory storage conditions are those which insure a free circulation of cool, dry air. Therefore, ventilation of the magazine is a very important point and should be so controlled that air will not be admitted when conditions on the inside of the magazine are such that condensation of moisture within the magazine would follow. The zinc-lined containers should be handled the least possible number of times, and whenever such handling is necessary it should be done with the greatest care, the object being to obviate any possibility of air leaks being produced in the containers.

(2) *Cleanliness.*—The important preliminary detail of cleanliness of the magazine floor should not be overlooked, for the accumulation of dirt, rubbish, and nails, aside from being unsightly, constitutes a menace. Scrapers should be placed at the door of the magazine so that mud, cinders, gravel, or other material will be removed from the shoes before the powder is stored. Under ordinary conditions it is not necessary to wear powder shoes in the magazine, except in the case of repacking, when it is advisable that this precaution be observed.

(3) *Location.*—Magazines must be so located that good drainage of the land is possible at all times. This is of special importance where large quantities of smokeless powder are being stored. In spite of the precaution observed for the elimination of leaky powder cans, the fact remains that there are many instances where the leaks are not discovered. This results, of course, in the powder in such cans absorbing moisture from the damp atmosphere in which it is stored, a condition very undesirable from the ballistic standpoint.

(4) *Fire precautions.*—The fire risk is not of serious consideration if the necessary precautions are observed. The danger of grass fire is practically nil if brush and undergrowth are removed from a distance of 50 feet around the building. Carrying matches or flash-producing devices of any kind should be strictly prohibited. This rule may be enforced by having those employees associated with

the storage depot searched for matches in their clothes at irregular intervals. Smoking, of course, should be absolutely forbidden at all times where explosives are manufactured, tested, or stored. Oil-burning lamps, lanterns, candles, etc., should be prohibited, and in those cases where artificial light is required special storage-battery lamps only should be used, or for short inspection the ordinary dry-battery flashlight.

*c. General safety regulations.*—(1) When it is necessary to renail boxes, nonsparking tools should be used. These consist of copper hammers, wooden mallets, copper nails, etc. Use of metal hooks for moving packages of high explosives or ammunition should not be permitted.

(2) When circumstances are such that it is impossible to get explosives under cover, a tarpaulin should be thrown over the exposed material, but in the event that an explosive becomes damp from inclement weather, it should be piled separately from the other explosives and a special chemical examination should be made of the wet material.

(3) Each magazine should be provided with a minimum and maximum thermometer, and careful record should be kept at all times of the variation in temperature.

(4) Except when material is being checked in or out of the magazine or during inventory, the building should be kept securely locked.

(5) Under no circumstances should packages of explosives or ammunition be opened within the magazine. If it is necessary to examine the material, it should be done outside of the building and far enough away so that in event of accident the building itself would not be endangered.

(6) Damaged packages should in every case be removed from the magazine and taken to a special repacking house before any attempt to salvage the material is made. If the damage is slight and a repacking house is not available, any repair or recoopering may be done outside at a distance not less than 100 feet from any magazine.

**26. Shipment.**—The transportation of explosives should be governed primarily by the rules of the Interstate Commerce Commission. These provide for the safety in transit of certain so-called acceptable explosives, provided that they comply in every way with the rules for packing and marking. Where shipment is in carload lots, each tier of boxes or containers must be carefully cleated and braced to provide against any possible misplacement through jar or shaking of the car.

SECTION V

## INSPECTION OF SMOKELESS POWDER

|                                    | Paragraph |
|------------------------------------|-----------|
| General                            | 27        |
| Testing raw materials              | 28        |
| DuPont nitrometer                  | 29        |
| Testing nitrocellulose             | 30        |
| Testing smokeless powder           | 31        |

**27. General.**—The foregoing consideration of the manufacture of smokeless powder emphasizes the prime importance of careful chemical supervision throughout the factory and demonstrates that standard methods of analysis are necessary if comparative results from different factories are to be of value. The purchase of the raw materials such as cotton, acids, alcohol, and diphenylamine is governed by specifications so designed that uniform quality of material will be obtained. As these specifications are necessarily of a chemical nature, it is essential that they prescribe in detail methods to be used in carrying out various tests and determinations. Methods of testing described in this manual are in general those prescribed in the latest U. S. Army specifications for the materials in question. In view, however, of the fact that the specifications are revised from time to time, reference should be made to the last revision of the specifications in order to obtain exact data as to approved methods.

**28. Testing raw materials.**—Methods for analysis of—

*a. Cellulose.*—(1) *Moisture.*—Not less than 3 grams (preferably 5 to 6 gr.) are weighed out in a ground glass covered moisture dish of suitable size, or an aluminum dish provided with a tight-fitting cover, and dried to constant weight in an oven at 105° C. (about 1½ hours). The dish is placed in a desiccator, covered, and when cool, weighed. The loss in weight is calculated to percent of moisture. At the same time that a sample is taken for moisture, a 2-gram sample is weighed out for the alkali soluble determination.

(2) *Extractive matter.*—The dried sample from the above moisture determination is placed in a Wiley or Soxhlet extractor and sufficient redistilled ethyl ether for the extraction is added. After the sample has been extracted on the steam bath for 3 hours the ether is transferred to a weighed beaker or evaporating dish and evaporated to dryness on a steam bath. The residue is heated for 30 minutes in an oven at 100° C., cooled in a desiccator, and weighed. From this the percent of extractible matter based on the dry cotton is calculated.

(3) *Ash.*—Approximately 2 grams of the sample are placed in a crucible and moistened with concentrated nitric acid and digested for about 1 hour on a steam bath or hot plate, then heated gently at first over a flame or in a muffle furnace until all combustible material is consumed. The crucible is then cooled in a desiccator and weighed. From the increase in weight the percent of ash is calculated on dry weight of sample.

(4) *Alkali soluble.*—The 2-gram sample of the cellulose weighed out with the moisture sample is used for the alkali soluble determination as follows: The sample is heated in a 250-cc. Erlenmeyer flask provided with a rubber stopper through which passes a long glass tube which serves as an air reflux, with 100 cc. of caustic soda solution (7.14 percent ±0.1 percent) for 3 hours at 100° C. After heating is completed the cellulose and solution are poured into a beaker containing a liter of distilled water. The alkali is neutralized with a decided excess of acetic acid. The undissolved cellulose is filtered within 5 minutes on a weighed Gooch crucible having an asbestos mat and thoroughly washed successively with hot water, alcohol, and ether. It is then dried rapidly to constant weight at 102° to 105° C. The loss is then calculated as percent alkali soluble on the dry weight of cellulose.

(5) *Lime, chlorides, and sulphates.*—A 5- to 10-gram sample is boiled for about ½ hour with approximately 100 cc. of distilled water. The water is then filtered off, a small portion slightly acidified with hydrochloric acid and brought to a boil. While hot, about 1cc. of 5- to 10-percent barium chloride solution is added. If only a faint cloudiness is noted the sample is considered as containing but a trace of sulphates. Another small portion of the water extract is taken and acidified slightly with nitric acid. A few drops of silver nitrate solution are added. If only a slight cloudiness is noted, the cellulose may be considered as containing but a trace of chlorides. Another small portion of the water extract is made slightly acid with hydrochloric acid and then faintly ammoniacal with ammonium hydroxide. A few cubic centimeters of a saturated solution of ammonium oxalate solution is added and the solution boiled. If but a faint cloudiness is noted without the formation of a precipitate the material may be considered as having but a trace of lime.

(6) *Hypochlorites.*—Approximately 1 gram of the sample is placed in a uniform layer on the bottom of a 150-cc. beaker. Ten cubic centimeters of a 10-percent solution of potassium iodide are poured carefully on the center of the moistened cellulose. A slight violet coloration indicates the presence of hypochlorites. The test is sensitive to about 0.01 percent.

(7) *Absorbency.*—The absorbency of the cellulose is determined by taking approximately 1 gram of the dried sample, rolling it into a ball in the palm of the hand, and placing it lightly on the surface of approximately 200 cc. of water in a 250-cc. beaker.  The ball will sink below the surface of the water within 10 seconds if the sample has satisfactory absorbent properties.

(8) *Viscosity.*—If the viscosity of the cellulose is specified in the contract, it is determined by the method given in the Journal of Industrial and Engineering Chemistry, Analytical Edition (see par. 89).

*b. Diphenylamine.*—(1) *Color.*—A portion of the sample of diphenylamine is ground to pass a 10-mesh screen (opening, 0.065 in.). The color is determined by visual examination of the ground material and should not be darker than a light brown.

(2) *Setting point.*—From 80 to 100 grams of the sample are ground to pass a 10-mesh screen after which the ground sample is dried for 4 hours at 40° C.   In lieu of drying the molten sample may be mixed with 20 grams of anhydrous calcium chloride or sodium sulphate, and the mixture stirred for 15 minutes at a temperature of 80° C., after which the mineral salts are allowed to settle and the molten diphenylamine poured off.  The dried sample is transferred to the inner tube of a solidification point apparatus and melted.  This tube is then placed in the apparatus and a standard thermometer is so adjusted that the bulb is in the center of the diphenylamine with a side thermometer in position for the emergent stem correction.  The molten material is vigorously stirred by means of the hand stirrer and the point at which the temperature begins to rise is carefully noted.  When solidification begins, the temperature is recorded every 15 seconds until a maximum reading is obtained.  The maximum temperature reading is corrected for the emergent stem by adding the value calculated from the formula

$$N \ (T\text{-}t) \times 0.000159$$

where  $N$ = Degrees in exposed mercury column.

$t$ = Average temperature of exposed mercury column determined by means of a second thermometer suspended so that its bulb is in the midpoint of exposed mercury column.

$T$ = Uncorrected setting point.

0.000159 = Coefficient of expansion of mercury in glass.

The corrected reading is recorded as the setting point of the sample and should fall within a range of 51.7° C. to 53° C.

(3) *Solubility.*—Twenty-five grams of the sample are dissolved in 100 cc. of ethyl ether of a specific gravity 0.717 to 0.723 at 20°/20° C. This solution is filtered through a tared Gooch crucible and washed thoroughly with additional solvent. The crucible is then dried at a temperature of 100° C., cooled in a desiccator, and weighed. The percentage of insoluble matter is then calculated and should not exceed 0.02 percent.

(4) *Moisture.*—Three to five grams of the powdered sample are weighed in a tared weighing bottle of about 5-cm. diameter. The weighed sample is heated for 4 hours at 40° C. or placed in a sulphuric acid desiccator at room temperature for 24 hours. The loss in weight calculated in percent is recorded as the percent moisture and should not exceed 0.2 percent.

(5) *Acid or alkali.*—Twenty grams of the ground sample are placed in a 250-cc. Erlenmeyer flask and 50 cc. of nearly boiling distilled water added. The flask is immediately stoppered and shaken vigorously for about 10 minutes. It is then cooled to 25° C. and the solution filtered, retaining the diphenylamine in the flask. This extraction is repeated with 50 cc. of hot water. A few drops of phenolphthalein are added to the filtrate, after which it is titrated with 0.1 N alkali if acid, or 0.1 N acid if alkaline. A blank determination is made on the water and used as a correction in the titration of diphenylamine for any acidity or alkalinity found. The acidity or alkalinity is calculated to hydrochloric acid or sodium hydroxide as the case may be. The sample should not contain more than 0.005 percent of free and combined acid or alkali. The filtrate on this determination is reserved for the determination of aniline.

(6) *Aniline and aniline salts.*—The filtrate from the acid or alkali determination is used for the determination of aniline or aniline salts present. The bromide-bromate method used for this determination is as follows: The filtrate is transferred to a glass-stoppered Erlenmeyer flask and 25 cc. of 0.1 N bromide-bromate water solution are added by means of an accurate 25-cc. pipette. The bromide-bromate solution contains 2.784 grams of $KBrO_3$ and 15 grams of KBr per liter. The mixture is cooled to 15° C. and 5 cc. of concentrated hydrochloric acid are added. After 1 minute, 10 cc. of 10-percent of potassium iodide solution are added. The contents of the flask are then titrated with 0.1 N sodium thiosulphate solution using starch as an indicator. A blank determination is made on 25 cc. of the bromide-bromate solution exactly as described above. In calculating the results, correction is made for the amount of diphenylamine dissolved in 100 cc. of water at 25° C. by subtracting 0.33 cc. from the

number of cubic centimeters of normal thiosulphate solution representing the difference between the blank and sample titrations.

Calculation: Percent of aniline=

$$\frac{((A\text{-}B)N\text{-}0.33)\ (0.01551)\ (100)}{W}$$

A=cc. of $Na_2S_2O_3$ solution used in blank titration.
B=cc. of $Na_2S_2O_3$ solution used in sample titration.
N=Normality of $Na_2S_2O_3$ solution.
W=Weight of sample taken.

The amount of free aniline or aniline salts contained in the sample will not exceed 0.1 percent, calculated as $C_6H_5NH_2$.

*c. Mixed acids.*—(1) *Suspended matter.*—A portion of approximately 40 grams of the sample accurately weighed from an acid-weighing bottle is filtered through a tared Gooch crucible containing a carefully prepared and dried asbestos mat. The mud or suspended material held on the asbestos mat is washed with at least five 20-c.c. portions of anhydrous alcohol. The anhydrous alcohol used may be prepared by allowing 95 percent alcohol denatured with 0.5 percent of benzene to stand over anhydrous copper sulphate, and filtering the alcohol before use. The crucible is dried for 3 hours at 125° C., cooled in a desiccator, and weighed. The increase in weight of the crucible is calculated as percentage of suspended matter.

(2) *Ash.*—The filtrate obtained from the determination of suspended matter is placed in a tared platinum or silica dish, heated slowly with a Bunsen flame under a hood until the evolution of fumes has ceased, and then heated to a dull red for 2 or 3 minutes, cooled in a desiccator, and weighed. It is heated for a further short period to determine if constant weight has been obtained. The increase in weight of the dish is calculated as percentage of ash.

(3) *Total acidity.*—By means of a Lunge acid-weighing pipette, a carefully weighed portion of approximately 1.5 grams of the sample is carefully transferred to a 500-cc. Erlenmeyer flask containing about 50 cc. of distilled water. Two or three drops of phenolphthalein or methyl red indicator are added and the solution titrated with standardized N/2 or N/3 sodium hydroxide solution. The total acidity is calculated in terms of sulphuric acid after subtracting from the weight of mixed acid the weights of suspended matter and ash calculated to be present.

(4) *Total nitric acid.*—About 5 cc. of special nitrogen-free sulphuric acid (94.5±0.5 percent) are placed in the cup of the gener-

ating bulb of the DuPont nitrometer. There is rapidly introduced a known weight of the sample of mixed acid, estimated to contain approximately 0.50 to 0.55 gram of nitric acid into the cup, the acid being stirred by means of a small glass rod. As soon as the mixed acid has been added, the stopcocks of the acid pipette are closed and the cap on the pipette quickly replaced and the acid in the cup drawn into the generating bulb. Four 5-cc. portions of the sulphuric acid are used to wash thoroughly the sample into the generating bulb, making a total consumption of 25 cc. of sulphuric acid used in the test. It is customary to reweigh the pipette with as little delay as possible after the first washing with 5 cc. of sulphuric acid to minimize any evaporation losses or absorption of moisture from the air. When the sample has been completely drawn into the generating bulb, the upper stopcock is closed, the lower stopcock allowed to remain open, and the mercury reservoir adjusted so as to give a slightly reduced pressure in the generating bulb. The bulb is shaken gently until most of the gas has been generated. The mercury reservoir is adjusted so that the mercury in the generating bulb drops nearly to the lower shoulder, and the lower stopcock closed. The bulb is shaken vigorously for 3 minutes. The bulb is replaced on the rack, with the lower stopcock open and the mercury reservoir adjusted until the mercury in the generating bulb is approximately the same height as the mercury in the reservoir. This adjustment is for the purpose of bringing the pressure inside of the generating bulb to approximately one atmosphere, so that the solubility of the nitric oxide gas in the sulphuric acid will not vary too widely. The lower stopcock is closed and the bulb shaken vigorously for an additional minute. The gas is transferred to the measuring tube and the levels of the mercury in the compensating tube and measuring tube adjusted to approximately the same height. The gas is allowed to stand for about 20 minutes in order to permit equalization of the temperature of the gas in the two tubes, the mercury levels are adjusted closely with a leveling device and the burette read. The percentage of total nitric acid is calculated by the formula

$$\text{Total nitric acid} = \frac{4.4975A}{B}$$

where A = reading on gas burette of nitrometer.
      B = weight of sample of acid taken minus weights of suspended matter and ash calculated to be present.

(5) *Oxides of nitrogen.*—A known weight of approximately 10 grams of mixed acid is transferred to a 300-cc. Erlenmeyer flask

containing 75 cc. of distilled water.  A standardized 0.1N potassium permanganate solution is added at intervals with agitation until the end point is observed, indicated by a permanent delicate pink coloration.  The percentage of oxides of nitrogen is calculated as nitrogen dioxide by the formula

$$\text{Oxides of nitrogen} = \frac{4.601\text{AB}}{\text{C}}$$

where A = Number of cc. $KMnO_4$ solution used.
      B = Normality factor of the $KMnO_4$ solution.
      C = Weight of sample taken minus weights of suspended matter and ash calculated to be present.

(6) *Sulphuric acid.*—The sulphuric acid content of the mixed acid free from suspended matter and ash is calculated as follows:

    Sulphuric acid = A − 0.77816B
where           A = Total acidity, expressed as sulphuric acid.
              B = Total nitric acid.

(7) *Nitric acid.*—The nitric acid content of the mixed acid free from suspended matter and ash is calculated as follows:

          Nitric acid = A − 1.3695B
where           A = Total nitric acid.
           B = Oxides of nitrogen.

(8) *Water.*—The water content of the mixed acid free from suspended matter and ash is calculated by subtracting from 100 percent the sum of the percentages of sulphuric acid, nitric acid, and oxides of nitrogen.

If it is desired, a Gooch crucible with an asbestos mat may be substituted for the filter paper if the mat is thick and compact, and the operator can check results by this method with those by the method described above.

*d. Ethyl alcohol.*—(1) *Content.*—The specific gravity at 20°/4° C. is determined by means of a calibrated hydrometer or pycnometer. The percentage of alcohol by volume is obtained by reference to the tables of the Official and Tentative Methods of Analyses of the Association of Official Agricultural Chemists.  (See par. 89).

(2) *Acidity.*—50 cc. of neutral distilled water is placed in a 250-cc. Erlenmeyer flask and a 50-cc. portion of the sample added measured by means of a graduated cylinder.  Six drops of gallein indicator (made by dissolving 1 gram of gallein in 1 liter of neutral ethyl alcohol, approximately 95 percent by volume) are added and titrated with approximately tenth-normal sodium hydroxide or potassium

hydroxide solution. The percentage of acidity in the sample is calculated:

$$\text{Percentage of acidity as acetic acid} = \frac{0.12 \ AB}{C}$$

where A=cc. of hydroxide solution.
B=Normality of hydroxide solution.
C=Specific gravity of alcohol.

(3) *Residue.*—A 100-cc. portion of the sample, measured by means of a pipette, is transferred to a tared evaporating dish. The liquid is evaporated on a steam bath to dryness, then dried for 2 hours at 100° C., cooled in a desiccator, and weighed. The increase in weight of the dish is calculated to percentage of residue.

$$\text{Percentage of residue} = \frac{A}{B}$$

where A=Weight of residue.
B=Specific gravity of sample.

(4) *Aldehyde.*—Silver nitrate and sodium hydroxide solutions are prepared containing 9 grams of compound per 100 cc. of distilled water. By means of a pipette 1 cc. of the silver nitrate solution and 1 cc. of the sodium hydroxide solution are transferred to a graduated cylinder (5–10 cc. capacity) and approximately 1 cc. of ammonium hydroxide (sp. gr. .90), or an amount sufficient to dissolve the precipitate formed by addition of the sodium hydroxide to the silver nitrate solution is added. By means of a pipette or burette, a 10-cc. portion of the sample is transferred to a clean, glass-stoppered bottle or flask and 1 cc. of the solution from the graduated cylinder added. The bottle is shaken well and allowed to remain in a dark place for 1 hour. The solution is filtered and the clear filtrate tested for unreduced silver by adding 1 cc. of a 10-percent solution of sodium chloride. If any precipitate is formed as shown by the cloudiness of the liquid, it is indicated that the alcohol contains not more than a trace of aldehyde. When the test is completed the solutions used are destroyed, as a sensitive silver salt may be formed.

(5) *Fusel oils, etc.*—Both of the following tests are made:

(a) By means of a graduated cylinder, a 10-cc. portion of the sample is transferred to a clean, clear test tube. One cc. of a solution made by dissolving 1 gram of potassium permanganate in 1 liter of distilled water is added. If the color of the mixture turns yellow in 20 minutes, fusel oils or other organic impurities are indicated to be present.

(b) By means of a graduated cylinder, a 10-cc. portion of the sample is transferred to a clean, clear test tube. Ten cc. of C. P.

sulphuric acid (sp. gr., 1.84) is added. If a yellow color results, the presence of organic impurities is indicated.

(6) *Benzene.*—By means of a graduated cylinder, a 100-cc. portion of the sample and 200 cc. of distilled water are transferred to a 1-liter side-neck distillation flask fitted with a straight glass condenser having a water jacket approximately 40 cm. long, 35 mm. diameter, and a 10-mm. central tube. The mixture is distilled at a rate of 1.0 to 1.5 cc. per minute and 20 cc. ±0.10 cc. collected in a suitable graduated container. If it is thought because of a cloudy appearance of the mixture after dilution with the water that the benzene content exceeds 0.75 percent, an additional 10 cc. of the distillate is collected in a separate container. The first 20 cc. of the distillate collected is transferred to the receiving bulb of the benzenometer. To this distillate 15.0±0.10 cc. of a 2.5- to 3.0-percent solution of potassium dichromate and 3.0±0.1 cc. of hydrochloric acid (sp. gr. 1.20) are added from a burette. The bulb is closed with a well-fitting straight-sided rubber stopper, shaken for 2 to 3 minutes, and allowed to stand for 15 minutes or until an olive-green color develops, indicating complete oxidation of the alcohol to acetic acid. It is important that the oxidation be complete, otherwise values that are too high may be obtained. The solution is carefully drawn into the graduated tube and lower bulb by slowly lowering the mercury reservoir. After about 15 minutes when the drainage of the liquid from the walls of the receiving bulb is complete, the exact volume of the liquid is read which is approximately 37 cc. The volume of the tube and the lower bulb from the mark on the bottom of the lower bulb to the zero mark on the tube is 37.5 cc. If the volume of the liquid is not within 0.5 cc. of the zero mark, sufficient dichromate solution is added to increase the volume to 37.0 cc. The mercury reservoir is slowly raised until all of the solution has been transferred to the receiving bulb and 10 cc. of petroleum ether is added. The rubber stopper is inserted in the mouth of the receiving bulb and shaken thoroughly for 2 or 3 minutes. The mercury reservoir is slowly lowered until the mercury with glass tube is level with the mark below the lower bulb. It is allowed to stand for at least ½ hour in order to effect complete separation of two layers of aqueous solution and petroleum ether, and the decrease in volume of the aqueous solution caused by the extraction of the benzene by the petroleum ether is noted. If the 10-cc. additional distillate is collected, it is treated in exactly the same manner as the 20-cc. portion, and the values obtained added. A blank determination is made on the same

amount of absolute alcohol as of distillate used (20 cc. or 30 cc.) and a correction made, if any is found.

*e. Ether.*—(1) *Color.*—Visual comparison is made of the ether and water in test tubes of 25-cc. capacity.

(2) *Nonvolatile residue.*—100 cc. of the sample is transferred to a tared beaker or evaporating dish, evaporated to dryness on a steam bath, and dried at 100° C. for 1 hour. This is cooled in a desiccator and weighed. The gain in weight is calculated as percentage of non-volatile residue as follows:

$$\text{Percentage of nonvolatile residue} = \frac{\text{Weight residue}}{\text{Specific gravity}}$$

The specific gravity is determined by means of a standardized hydrometer, Westphal balance, or a specific-gravity bottle, and expressed as specific gravity at 20° C./20° C.

(3) *Acidity.*—Fifty cc. of alcohol are placed in an Erlenmeyer flask, five drops of phenolphthalein added, and neutralized with approximately 0.1N sodium-hydroxide solution. One hundred cc. of the ether is added, mixed, and titrated with the standard alkali to a faint pink.

**29. DuPont nitrometer.**—*a. Theoretical.*—The DuPont nitrometer is a modification of the Lunge nitrometer and is devised to avoid necessity of making the usual correction for temperature and barometric pressure which must be calculated with every gas measurement. The principle of the apparatus is to inclose a known volume of air at such a pressure that it takes up exactly the volume which it would occupy at 20° C. and 760 mm. pressure. If the same pressure and temperature are then applied to another volume of gas this will also take up the volume which it would occupy at 20° C. and 760 mm. pressure. The volume of air is kept in a "compensating tube" which is connected with the reading tube of the nitrometer. When it is desired to read the volume of a given quantity of NO gas at 20° C. and 760 mm. pressure, the level of the mercury in the compensating tube is brought to the mark at which the air within the tube occupies the space it would occupy at 20° C. and 760 mm. pressure, the level of the mercury in the reading tube is brought to the same level as the mark, and the reading made. The reading tube of the DuPont nitrometer is graduated to read directly the percentage of nitrogen when a 1-gram sample is used.

*b. Assembly.*—The various tubes are arranged on the nitrometer rack in order shown in figure 28; 25 cc. of 94 to 95 percent $H_2SO_4$ is then placed in No. 2 and a quantity of air drawn in through the stopcock. The stopcock is then closed and the bulb shaken vigorously to dry the air. The shaking is repeated several times at intervals of from 10 to 15 minutes. When the air is judged to be thoroughly dry, 2 and 4 are connected and the dry air run into 4 until, with the stopcock of 3 open and the mercury in 3, 4, and 5, on the same level, the reading in 3 is about 12.50. No. 4 is then sealed with a small blowpipe flame. Another portion of air is then desiccated in 2 and transferred to 3 until, with the mercury in 3, 4, and 5 on the same level, the reading in 3 is about 12.50. It is not necessary that these gas volumes be exact or equal. The small manometer, A, is then filled with $H_2SO_4$ and attached to 3. The apparatus is then left to come to constant temperature. The mercury in 3, 4, and 5 is then adjusted so that the air in 3 is under atmospheric pressure as shown by the acid in A. The reading is taken on the graduated scale on 3. The temperature and barometric pressure are noted at the same time. From these readings the volume of air in 3 is calculated at 20° C. and 760 mm. pressure by the gas laws which are expressed by the equation:

$$V : V' = P' : P$$
$$V : V' = T : T'$$

in which $V$ = Volume at 20° C. and 760 mm.

$V'$ = Volume at the observed temperature $T'$ and pressure $P'$.

From these is derived the equation:

$$V = V' \frac{P' \times 293 \times (1 - 0.00018t')}{760 \times (273 + T') \times (1 - 0.00018 \times 20)}$$

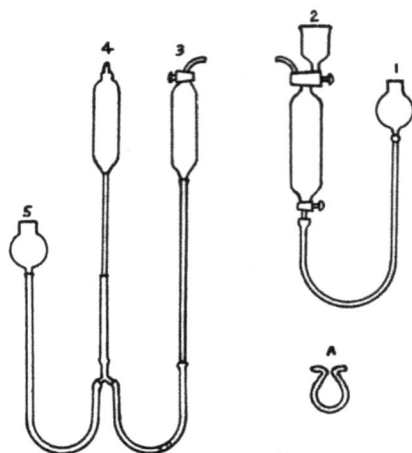

FIGURE 28.—Nitrometer.

The last term of the equation represents the correction to be applied for the coefficient of expansion of mercury in the barometer where t' equals temperature of the barometer. When V has been calculated, the mercury in 3, 4, and 5 is adjusted so that with the mercury in 3 and 4 on a level the mercury in 3 marks the calculated volume of air. The height of the mercury in 4 is then marked by a strip of paper pasted on the tube. This is taken as the standard volume with which every volume of gas to be measured is compared.

c. *Standardization with C. P. KNO₃.*—A sample of C. P. $KNO_3$ which has been recrystallized three times from 95 percent alcohol is finely ground and dried for 2 to 3 hours at 135° to 150° C. Exactly 1 gram is weighed out into a small weighing bottle and transferred to the nitrometer (for details see par. 30*d*), dissolving the $KNO_3$ in the nitrometer cup with 20 cc. of 94.5 percent ± 0.5 percent $H_2SO_4$. With the lower stopcock of the generating bulb open and the mercury bulb low enough to give a reduced pressure in 2, the generating bulb is gently shaken until the larger portion of gas has been generated. The generating bulb is then raised until the mercury drops nearly to the lower shoulder, the lower stopcock closed, and the bulb is shaken vigorously for 3 minutes. After replacing on the rack, the lower cock is opened and the bulb allowed to stand for several minutes. The lower stopcock is closed and the shaking is then repeated for an additional 3 minutes, adjusting the mercury as before. Finally the gas is transferred to 3, the positions of 3, 4, and 5 so adjusted that the level of mercury in 3 and 4 is about the same and the apparatus allowed to stand 20 minutes. The mercury levels are then carefully adjusted with a leveling device and the reading in 3 taken. This should be 13.85 percent.

d. *Standardization by test blend.*—This standardization is run in a way similar to *c* above except that a blend of nitrocellulose which has been carefully tested on a standardized nitrometer is used. This method is somewhat more convenient than the method with $KNO_3$ because the nitrocellulose is more easily broken up in the nitrometer than $KNO_3$. Whenever a doubt exists, however, the standardization must be carried out with $KNO_3$.

**30. Testing nitrocellulose.**—*a. Solubility.*—(1) *In ether-alcohol.*—The official temperature for this determination is 15.5° C., and in any case where the material does not comply with the specification or where greater accuracy is desired, the complete determination is made at this temperature, the solvents being brought to this temperature before their addition to the sample. Nitrocellulose is more soluble at 15.5° C. than at a higher temperature. Ether and alcohol used should be of the quality prescribed for use in manufacture of smokeless powder.

*Volumetric method.*—One gram of the dry sample is placed in an Erlenmeyer flask and 75 cubic centimeters of alcohol added, shaken thoroughly for about five minutes and allowed to stand for two hours. One hundred and fifty cubic centimeters of ether are then added and the mixture thoroughly shaken and allowed to stand stoppered overnight. It is desirable to start this determination early in the day in order to give it plenty of agitation before standing overnight, as agitation facilitates solution.

The process used in the remainder of the determination depends upon the grade of nitrocellulose being tested, on account of the variation in the solubility of the different grades.

In the case of pyrocellulose, the mixture in the flask is thoroughly shaken the next morning and transferred to a special solubility tube of the following dimensions: Total length, 21 inches; inside diameter, 1.35 inches; the lower end constricted for a length of 2 inches to an inside diameter of 0.3 inches and graduated in one-tenth cubic centimeter. The constricted portion should be tapered gradually from the large part of the tube. After standing in the solubility tube until the insoluble material has settled completely as indicated by the volume of this material remaining constant over a period of one hour, the volume occupied by the insoluble and semisolid matter is read in cubic centimeters from the scale on the tube. If the reading is 0.25 cubic centimeter or less, the percentage of insoluble is considered to be 1 percent or less. Should the reading exceed 0.25 cubic centimeter, the gravimetric method will be used as follows:

*Gravimetric method.*—The clear liquid in the solubility tube obtained as above is siphoned off to about one-fourth inch from the upper surface of the settled residue, then alcohol is added to one-third the capacity of the tube, shaken vigorously and ether added to about 3 inches of the top, shaken and allowed to settle. This process of washing by decantation is repeated four times, and after the fourth decantation the insoluble residue is completely washed into a beaker with a small quantity of ether-alcohol solution. The contents of the beaker are filtered through a weighed Gooch crucible with ignited asbestos mat, washed free from soluble nitrocellulose with ether-alcohol solution, dried at a low temperature until no odor of ether can be detected and then at 100° C. to constant weight, cooled, and weighed. The crucible is then carefully ignited over a free flame, cooled, and weighed again. The loss of weight on ignition is considered as the insoluble nitrocellulose.

In the case of guncotton or blends of pyrocellulose and guncotton, 100 cubic centimeters of the clear solution is drawn from the solubility tube (without disturbing the settled layer of insoluble material) and run into an aluminum can 50 millimeters in height by 90 millimeters in diameter, with tightly fitting cover, which has previously been dried and weighed. The soluble nitrocellulose is now precipitated from the clear solution in the can by the addition of distilled water. A finely divided precipitate of fibrous appearance is desired, and is best obtained by first heating the solution on a steam hot plate (the tared aluminum can should not come in contact with steam or hot water) to evaporate part of the ether, then adding about 50 cc. of distilled water gradually with continued heating and stirring. The exact procedure for obtaining the best results must be determined by experience. After the nitrocellulose has been precipitated, heating is continued until the liquid is evaporated just to dryness. The can with contents is then dried in an oven at 95° to 100° C. for 1½ hours, cooled in a desiccator, and weighed. A check weight should be obtained after additional drying for ½ hour. The increase in weight of the can is the weight of soluble nitrocellulose. The percentage of the latter is calculated as follows:

$$\text{Percent soluble nitrocellulose} = \frac{A}{B} 100$$

Where    $A$ = Weight of soluble nitrocellulose in 100 cc. of clear solution.

$B$ = ⅘ of weight of original sample.

(2) *In acetone.*—This is determined by the same method as the solubility in ether-alcohol, except that acetone is used as solvent. If the volumetric reading is greater than 0.2, the determination is made gravimetrically.

*b. K. I. starch test.*—The sample is pressed in a clean cloth or wrung out in a wringer if it contains a large excess of water. The cake is rubbed up in the cloth until fine, taking care that it does not come in contact with the hands, spread out on clean paper trays, and dried in the air bath at 35° to 40° C. until the proper moisture content has been obtained. The desired moisture content is that which will give condensation of moisture in diminishing amounts in the five test tubes used, ranging from an appreciable amount in the first tube to none in the fifth as the test progresses. The proper condition of nitrocellulose for the first sample is indicated when the nitrocellulose clings, after rubbing, to a spatula or tissue paper which has been wrapped about the fingers. A sample of 1.3 grams is weighed out on a dispensing balance and transferred to a tube. More tubes are filled approximately at 4- to 5-minute intervals until five tubes have been prepared. The tubes used should be 5½ inches long, ½ inch internal diameter, and ⅝ inch external diameter. During the test the tubes are closed by a clean, tight-fitting cork stopper through which passes a tight-fitting glass rod equipped with a platinum holder for the paper. Corks are discarded after one test. The nitrocellulose is pressed or shaken down in the tube until it occupies a space of 1⅝ inches. The test paper, about 1 inch in length and ⅜ inch wide, is hung on the platinum holder, and moistened on its upper half with a 50-percent solution of pure glycerin in water. The heating bath is carefully regulated at 65.5° C. ±1°, and is placed so that a bright reflected light is obtained. The time is taken when the tubes enter the bath. As the test continues, the line of demarcation between wet and dry test paper is kept abreast the lower edge of the moisture film. The first appearance of discoloration of the damp portion of the test paper marks the end of the test for each separate tube, the minimum test of any one of the five tubes being the heat test of the nitrocellulose. This discoloration is to be greater than that obtained at the same time by a blank test. Standard test paper is used in this test and is furnished by the Government. The standard water bath holds 10 tubes and is made long and narrow to reduce to a minimum the heating of the upper portions of the tubes. The tubes are immersed in the bath to a standard depth of 2.25 inches.

  c. *Heat test at 134.5° C.*—A sample of nitrocellulose is laid out in paper trays and dried for 4 or 5 hours at about 40° C., or is dried over night at room temperature and then further dried ½ hour at about 40° C., after which 2.5 grams are pressed into the lower 2 inches in each of two tubes of heavy glass about 290 mm. long, 18 mm. outside diameter, and 15 mm. inside diameter, closed with a cork stopper through which a hole or notch 4 mm. in diameter has been bored or cut. A piece of standard normal methyl violet paper, 70 mm. long and 20 mm. wide, is placed in each tube, its lower edge 25 mm. above the sample. When the constant temperature bath has been carefully regulated at 134.5° C. ± 0.5° C., these tubes are placed in the bath so that no more than 6 or 7 mm. of length project from bath. Examination of the tube is made by withdrawing about one-half its length and replacing quickly each 5 minutes after 20 minutes have elapsed. The minimum time, which will be a multiple of 5, in which the violet color of the test paper in either tube has completely turned to salmon pink will be reported as the time of test. For example, if the violet color is not completely changed in 25 minutes but is completely changed in 30 minutes, the time of the test is recorded as 30 minutes. The bath must be placed in a good light, with a suitable background. The standard normal methyl violet paper is furnished by the Government.

*d. Determination of nitrogen.*—A sample of approximately 1 gram of nitrocellulose air-dried at a temperature not above 46° C. is placed in a ground glass stoppered weighing bottle (dimensions, approximately 50 mm. high by 25 mm. diameter) and dried for 1½ hours at a temperature ranging from 98° to 102° C., cooled in a desiccator, and weighed. The standard DuPont 5-part form of Lunge's nitrometer with properly standardized compensating and reading tubes is used for determination of nitrogen. For standard operation room temperature must be between 15° and 32° C. The cup of the generating bulb is washed free from any nitrogenous impurities and the nitrocellulose transferred to the cup; 20 cc. of nitrogen-free sulphuric acid, strength 94.5 ± 0.5 percent is measured out into a graduate or small beaker. Small portions of the acid are run into the weighing bottle and transferred to the generating bulb until a sufficient quantity has been used to make an emulsion with the nitrocellulose. The mercury reservoir is lowered sufficiently to cause reduced pressure in the generating bulb. The upper stopcock is opened wide and the lower opened sufficiently to draw the nitrocellulose into the generating bulb. Successive rinsings with sulphuric acid are made until all of the nitrocellulose has been drawn in with the 20 cc. of acid. The upper stopcock is generally manipulated after the first time. Any air drawn into the bulb should be forced out, after which the upper stopcock is closed, the lower one remaining open, and the mercury reservoir adjusted just low enough to give a slightly reduced pressure in the generating bulb. The generating bulb is shaken gently, keeping the lower end in a fixed position until most of the gas has been generated. The mercury reservoir is adjusted so that the mercury in the generating bulb drops nearly to the lower shoulder, whereupon the lower stopcock is closed and the bulb shaken vigorously for 3 minutes. The bulb is replaced on the rack with the lower stopcock open and the mercury reservoir adjusted until the mercury in the generating bulb is approximately the same height as the mercury in the reservoir. This adjustment is for the purpose of bringing the pressure inside of the generating bulb to approximately one atmosphere so that the solubility of the nitric oxide gas in the sulphuric acid will not vary too widely. The lower stopcock is closed and the bulb shaken vigorously for an additional 3 minutes. The gas is now transferred to the measuring tube and the levels of the mercury in the compensating tube and the measuring tube are adjusted to approximately the same height. The gas is allowed to stand for about 20 minutes in order to permit equalization of temperature of the gas in the two tubes, and the mercury levels closely adjusted with a leveling device. The reading of the measuring tube is divided by the weight of the sample of nitrocellulose, giving the percent nitrogen in the nitrocellulose. The tare weight of the weighing bottle may be obtained before or after the test.

e. Ash.—Two grams of dried nitrocellulose are placed in a recently ignited and tared crucible and treated with sufficient acetone containing 5 percent castor oil (by volume) to gelatinize thoroughly the nitrocellulose. It is then ignited and allowed to burn without applying heat until a charred residue remains, and finally it is thoroughly ignited, cooled, weighed, and the percentage of ash calculated. If preferred, the nitrocellulose may be digested with nitric acid, ignited carefully, and the ash determined.

**31. Testing Smokeless Powder.**—*a. Samples.*—(1) *Ballistic.*—The number of containers required to make up the ballistic sample and the chemical and stability sample as prescribed in the specification should be selected so as to be representative of the lot. If the weight of the samples required is less than 10 containers, a portion equal to $\frac{1}{10}$ the weight of the required ballistic sample should be removed from each of 10 boxes and those 10 portions should be packed in individual airtight containers. It is desirable that the ballistic sample be taken not sooner than 2 weeks after the original packing.

(2) *Chemical and stability.*—From each of the containers sampled for the ballistic tests, there should be removed equal portions of the powder so as to have a sample for the chemical and stability tests of approximately the weight prescribed in the specification. Not less than 5 pounds of this sample should be set aside for 65.5° C. surveillance tests. The greatest cleanliness should be observed in handling the chemical and stability sample and handling it with damp or soiled hands should be avoided. The sample should be mixed thoroughly.

*b. External moisture.*—(1) *Air-dried.*—A sample of about 20 grams of the powder (or 2 whole grains, if 1 grain weighs more than 10 grams) is weighed accurately in a tared glass weighing bottle. It is dried in a vacuum oven (vacuum of at least 25 inches of mercury) at 55±2° C. for 6 hours, cooled in a desiccator, and weighed. The loss in weight is calculated to percentage of moisture in the sample as received.

(2) *Water-dried.*—A sample of about 20 grams of the powder (or 2 whole grains if 1 grain weighs more than 10 grams) is weighed accurately in a tared glass weighing bottle. It is dried for 6 hours at $100\pm2°$ C. at atmospheric pressure, cooled in a desiccator, and weighed. The loss in weight is calculated to percentage of moisture in the sample as received.

*c. Diphenylamine.*—A sample of 5 grams of the powder is weighed accurately into a 250-cc. lipped beaker. The sample may be in whole grains if small enough to give a fair sample or in slices of medium or larger grains. Ten cc. of glacial acetic acid and 20 cc. of nitric acid (sp. gr. 1.42) are mixed and poured on the powder. The beaker is covered with a watch glass and placed on a steam bath at about 95° C. for 1½ hours. It is necessary that the above quantities of acid be strictly adhered to by using either a pipette or graduate for the measurement. The powder dissolves completely with copious evolution of red fumes. The time and temperature given allows all red fumes to be dissipated without too much reduction of volume, and this is the end to be attained as the nitro compounds have a tendency to crystallize out if the solution is evaporated too much or is allowed to stand too long after removal from the steam bath. Whenever such crystallization occurs results are slightly low.

Immediately after heating on the steam bath is completed, the solution is cooled, being careful not to agitate, and poured into 75 cc. of distilled water which has been cooled to 15° C. in a 250-cc. glass-stoppered Erlenmeyer flask. The beaker is washed with water so that the solution including washings will be approximately 120 cc. The flask is shaken well for about 2 minutes and allowed to stand overnight.

The nitro compound is filtered on a Gooch crucible prepared by washing with 10 percent nitric acid and igniting. The nitro compound is washed six or seven times with water containing 1 percent of nitric acid, dried at 100° to 105° C. for 1 hour, cooled in a desiccator, and weighed. The crucible is placed in a small beaker, 10 cc. of acetone added, and allowed to soak for 15 minutes. The crucible is placed on a suction flask and washed with small quantities of acetone until nitro compounds are completely removed. The crucible is dried at 100° to 105° C. for 1 hour, cooled in a desiccator, and weighed. The loss in weight is calculated as nitro compounds.

The factor for conversion of nitro compound to diphenylamine, using the quantities of acid stated above, is 0.4259.

$$\text{Percent diphenylamine} = \frac{\text{Weight of nitro compound} \times 0.4259 \times 100}{\text{Weight of powder}}$$

d. *Graphite.*—The crucible used for the determination of diphenylamine is placed in a muffle furnace or in an inclined position over a gas burner and heated strongly until all carbonaceous material has disappeared. The crucible is cooled in a desiccator and weighed. The loss in weight is calculated as percentage of graphite in the sample as received.

e. *Total volatiles.*—The volatile determination is started as soon after receipt of the sample as possible. Any grains which have been handled should not be returned to the sample, except in special cases where the sample available is very small. The sample container is kept tightly closed. About 20 grains of all powders are used regardless of caliber. A total of at least 2 grams is cut, taking approximately the same number of slices from each grain, after first cutting off and discarding about ¼ of the grain so that the slices used come from approximately midway between end and center of the grain. Each slice is cut so as to have as nearly as possible the same thickness at all parts of its area. The slices are cut either clear across the grain giving a circular area, or just half across giving a semicircular area. A sample of about 1 gram is weighed accurately into a tared aluminum can, approximately 50 mm. high and 90 mm. in diameter, provided with a tight fitting lid and an aluminum stirring rod, the weight of which is included in the weight of the can. This is treated with 50 cc. of alcohol complying with U. S. Army Specification No. 4–1018, and 100 cc. of ether complying with U. S. Army Specification No. 50–11–45. This should be stirred frequently if it is desired to hasten solution, or covered and the can left under a bell jar overnight. When solution is complete the ether that has evaporated is replaced. The can is placed on a steam box or on a closed steam bath and a portion of the ether evaporated. The aluminum can should not be permitted to come in contact with steam or hot water. The amount of ether evaporated before the precipitation of the nitrocellulose determines the character of the precipitate; if too much ether is evaporated the precipitate will be gummy and difficult to dry; if too little ether is evaporated the precipitate will be sandy and cause bumping. The amount of ether to evaporate in order to obtain the desired fine, flaky precipitate depends upon the amount of nitrocellulose present and can be learned only by practice. When it is considered that the correct amount of ether has been evaporated,

10 cc. of distilled water is added. If the solution becomes opaque indicating that the precipitation has started, water is added slowly with constant stirring to make a total of 50 cc. If the 10-cc. portion of water does not start the precipitation, a little more ether is evaporated and again 10 cc. of water is added. This process is repeated until a 10-cc. portion of water starts the precipitation and the precipitation is finished by adding sufficient water to make a total of 50 cc. If the precipitate seems too heavy, 5 cc. portions of ether are added and stirred until the precipitate becomes light and flaky. The ether is evaporated with constant stirring until there is no further danger of bumping and then just to dryness. The can is transferred to an oven at 95° to 100° C. and dried for 1½ hours, cooled in a desiccator, and weighed. The can is returned to the oven for ½ hour, cooled in a desiccator, and weighed. If the latter weighing does not check the former within 0.0005 gram, the ½-hour dryings in the oven are repeated until the results check within this limit. A nonvolatile residue at 95° to 100° C. is run on the quantities of water, alcohol, and ether used and the percentage of total volatiles is calculated as follows:

$$\text{Percentage of total volatiles} = \frac{(A-B+C-D\times100)}{E}$$

where A = Original weight of can and sample.
B = Final weight of can and sample.
C = Weight of water, ether, and alcohol residues.
D = Correction in grams for volatilization of diphenylamine during the determination. 25 percent of diphenylamine content of powder is allowed.
E = Original weight of sample.

The percentage of total volatiles, graphite, and diphenylamine is subtracted from 100 and reported as percentage of nitrocellulose in the sample.

  *f. Ash.*—From the remainder of the slices or grains a sample of about 1 gram is weighed accurately in a tared porcelain crucible. The sample is moistened with a small quantity of concentrated nitric acid and digested for 2 to 3 hours on a steam bath. The crucible is removed from steam bath and heated over a Bunsen burner cautiously at first to avoid loss. The crucible is finally placed in a muffle furnace, or in an inclined position partially covered with a lid over a gas burner, and heated strongly until all carbonaceous matter has disappeared, cooled in a desiccator, and weighed. From this weight the original weight of the crucible is subtracted and the result calculated as percent of ash in the sample as received.

*g. Compressibility.*—In this test grains which are abnormal in shape or contain óbvious flaws are not used. The ends of 10 normal grains of powder are cut so that new surfaces perpendicular to the length are exposed, and the length is equal to the diameter. The average length of these pieces is determined with a micrometer. Each grain is compressed between parallel surfaces, increasing the load slowly until the first crack appears. The load is removed and the grain measured. The average reduction in length is calculated in percentage of the average original length. If these 10 grains fail to pass this test, 20 more grains are subjected to the test. The average reduction in length is calculated in percentage of the average original length of the total 30 grains tested.

*h. Heat test at 134.5° C.*—Tests are made on five samples thus: 2.5 grams of sample are weighed out and each sample placed in a test tube made of heavy glass, preferably pyrex, approximately 15 mm. inside diameter, 18 mm. outside diameter, and 290 mm. long. Each sample should consist of as nearly whole grains as consistent with a weight of 2.5 grams of sample. In sectioning grains to obtain the required weight, the grains are split longitudinally. A piece of standard normal methyl violet paper, 70 mm. long and 20 mm. wide is placed vertically in each tube, its lower edge 25 mm. above the powder. The tubes are stoppered with corks through which holes 4 mm. in diameter have been bored. The tubes are placed in a constant temperature bath at 134.5±0.5° C. so that no more than 6 or 7 mm. of length project. Each tube is examined by withdrawing about one-half of its length and replacing quickly at 5-minute intervals after 55 minutes have elapsed. The time of the observation which reveals the test paper in any tube to be completely changed to a salmon pink color is recorded as the time of completion of the test. Heating is continued and report is made whether any sample of powder explodes in less than 5 hours. (Standard normal methyl violet papers and standards for salmon pink are secured from the Ordnance Department.)

*i. Dimensions.*—The form of grain is determined by visual examination.

(1) *Length.*—Thirty normal grains of powder are selected at random and the length measured with a micrometer. When the ends are irregular, the average length is determined as closely as possible.

(2) *Grain and perforation diameter, and web thickness.*—Ninety normal grains are selected of either single or multiperforated powder. By means of a razor blade or hacksaw each grain is cut partly through from opposite sides at about the middle, and broken under strain so that a narrow ridge of powder which includes the desired line of

measurement is left along the line of breakage. This desired line of measurement is a straight line forming a diameter of the grain which passes through the center of the perforation of a single perforated powder and through the centers of three perforations of a multi-perforated powder.

A number of the grains are placed vertically on a glass slide so that the broken ends are uppermost and the individual desired lines of measurement are in alinement. A film of vaseline is used on the glass slide to hold the grains in position if necessary. The slide is placed on the stage of a measuring microscope having a magnification of approximately 25 diameters, equipped with cross hairs, and having a horizontal scale and vernier screw scale capable of giving measurements accurate to 0.001 inch.

In case of multiperforated grains, the diameter of the grain, the two outer web thicknesses and two inner web thicknesses, and the diameters of three perforations of each of the 90 grains are measured by means of a continuous series of readings taken along the desired line of measurement of each grain. In the case of single perforated grains, the diameter of the grain, the two web thicknesses, and the diameter of the perforation of each of the 90 grains are measured by means of a continuous series of readings taken along the desired line of measurement of each grain.

(3) *Length-diameter ratio.*—From the measurements of length and grain diameter taken as described above, the ratio between the average length (L) and the average diameter (D) is calculated.

(4) *Length and diameter uniformity.*—From the measurement of length and grain diameter taken as described above, the mean variation of individual dimensions from the mean dimensions, expressed as percentage of the mean dimensions is calculated.

(5) *Grain diameter-perforation diameter ratio.*—From the measurements taken as described above, the ratio between the average grain diameter (D) and the average perforation diameter (d) is calculated.

*j. Web measurements.*—(1) *Type I.*—From the measurement made as described above, the average outer web thickness ($W_o$) and the average inner web thickness ($W_i$) for the 90 grains measured are calculated. The average web thickness ($W_a$) is calculated by taking the average of $W_o$ and $W_i$. The difference between the average outer web thickness ($W_o$) and the average inner web thickness ($W_i$) in terms of percentage of the average web thickness ($W_a$) is calculated.

$$\frac{(W_o - W_i) \times 100}{W_a} \text{ or } \frac{(W_i - W_o) \times 100}{W_a} = \text{percentage difference}$$

(2) *Type II.*—From the measurements made as described above, the average of the 90 web thicknesses above the median and the average of the 90 web thicknesses below the median are calculated. The percentage is calculated by which each of the two averages differs from the average of all the web measurements ($W_a$).

*k. Ballistic tests.*—(1) *Service velocity.*—The number of rounds prescribed in the specification are fired in the proper weapon with the prescribed projectiles with charges calculated to give the required service velocity. Powder from a different container is used for each round. In case the amount of powder required for a charge exceeds the contents of one box the charge is made up from as few containers as possible. The velocities and pressures developed are measured.

(2) *Velocity uniformity.*—The maximum variation and mean variation in the uniformity series are calculated.

(3) *Pressure.*—The mean pressure for the series is calculated. If the mean velocity obtained in the uniformity series is not equal to the prescribed service velocity, the charge that would be required to give the prescribed service velocity is estimated and the observed mean pressure corrected to the pressure that would have been obtained if the correct charge for obtaining the prescribed service velocity had been used.

(4) *Excess charge.*—With the prescribed projectile in the weapon for which the powder is intended, the number of excess charge rounds prescribed in the specification is fired, using a weight of charge 105 percent of the charge calculated to give the prescribed velocity. The maximum pressure developed for each is measured. In any case where the 105-percent charge exceeds the chamber capacity of the weapon, the excess charge should be as near 105 percent of the service charge as practicable.

SECTION VI

## COMPOUND PROPELLANTS

|  | Paragraph |
|---|---|
| General | 32 |
| Double base powders | 33 |
| E. C. powder | 34 |

**32. General.**—Discussion in preceding sections has been concerned largely with straight nitrocellulose powder, commonly referred to as pyro powder. There are some military weapons which require the use of propellants which have a greater potential than pyro powder, or which for special reasons are commonly provided with powders having compositions different from pyro powder. Various types of powder used for special purposes will be discussed briefly in this section. Other small-arms compound propellants used for military purposes will not be discussed in this manual as their composition and methods of manufacture cannot be described without disclosing information regarded by manufacturers as confidential.

**33. Double base powders.**—*a. Composition.*—The term "double base" powder has been applied to powders containing nitrocellulose and nitroglycerin as the principal constituents. These powders as used by various military services usually contain from 60 to 80 percent of nitrocellulose and from 40 to 20 percent nitroglycerin. Certain commercial powders used in sporting ammunition are of similar composition. The nitrocellulose used in double base powders may be of the pyrocellulose type containing about 12.6 percent nitrogen or the more highly nitrated type containing above 13.0 percent nitrogen, commonly referred to as guncotton. Small percentages of inorganic salts such as potassium or barium nitrate are often used in double base powders, these salts serving the purpose of reducing flash or rendering the powder more ignitible. When the percentage of nitroglycerin in the powder composition is small or when the powder is to be extruded, it is customary to use a volatile solvent to colloid the powder. With compositions containing a high percentage of nitroglycerin and which are granulated in thin sheets or discs by rolling, the volatile solvent may be omitted since nitroglycerin is in itself a solvent for nitrocellulose, and the rolling operation colloids the powder to the desired degree.

*b. Characteristics and use.*—The energy content of nitroglycerin is considerably higher than that for nitrocellulose and, therefore, powders containing nitroglycerin have higher potential than straight nitrocellulose powders, the difference increasing with the percent of nitroglycerin present. The double base powders are also more readily ignitible and have a higher rate of burning. These characteristics have led to the use of such powders in trench mortars where especially rapid burning is required. They are also used in certain high velocity weapons where the high potential of the double base powders is favorable.

*c. Inspection tests.*—(1) *General.*—In the inspection of the double base powders, the usual chemical stability, and ballistic tests are conducted. Since the chemical and ballistic test requirements vary with the various types of powder but the stability requirements are common to all, the latter requirements only are given in (2) below.

(2) *Heat test at 120° C.*—The heat test at 120° C. is used to determine stability. All powders are required to withstand this test for at least 40 minutes without changing the color of the test paper, and

to show no evidence of fumes in 60 minutes. The procedure for this test is as follows: 2.5 grams of the sample are placed in each of two tubes of heavy glass having the following approximate dimensions: length, 290 mm., outside diameter, 18 mm.; inside diameter, 15 mm. Each of the tubes is closed with a cork stopper through which has been cut a hole or groove of about 2-mm. diameter. A piece of standard normal methyl violet paper 70 mm. long and 20 mm. wide is placed in each tube so that its lower edge is 25 mm. above the powder. These tubes are placed in a bath at a temperature of 120.0 ±0.5° C. so that no more than 6 or 7 mm. of each tube project outside the bath. The tubes are examined by withdrawing about one-half their length outside the bath and replacing immediately. The tubes are examined every 5 minutes after the first 20 minutes have elapsed. The time in which the methyl violet paper has turned completely to standard salmon pink in either tube is reported. After 60 minutes the tubes are examined against a white background for evidence of fumes.

**34. E. C. Powder.**—*a. Composition and use.*—This propellant is generally used for loading blank cartridges and hand grenades. It consists of semicolloided nitrocellulose granulated with inorganic nitrates.

*b. Manufacture.*—The main point observed in manufacture is proper incorporation and mixing of all ingredients. This process is usually conducted by means of a wheel mill in a manner somewhat similar to that used for black powder. Nitrocellulose of approximately 13.15 percent nitrogen is mixed with about 16 percent of a mixture of equal parts of potassium nitrate and barium nitrate, together with a small amount of diphenylamine and a pink or yellow coloring matter. The powder mixture is granulated by adding a mixture of water and a suitable solvent to the material in a revolving drum in such a manner that it forms small rounded grains. The nitrocellulose in these grains is only partially colloided, acting as a binding material and hardening the surface of the grains as the solvent is removed.

*c. Granulation.*—The granulation of E. C. powder is such that the powder will pass a 12-mesh and remain on a 50-mesh screen. A tolerance of 3 percent is permitted, that is, 3 percent of the powder may remain on the 12-mesh screen, but the material remaining on the screen must pass a 10-mesh screen, and 3 percent may pass a 50-mesh screen.

*d. Heat test at 134.5° C.*—The powder must not turn normal methyl violet paper to a salmon pink color in less than 30 minutes and must not explode in less than 4 hours in this test.

Section VII

BLACK POWDER

| | Paragraph |
|---|---|
| General | 35 |
| Manufacture | 36 |
| Packing | 37 |
| Inspection | 38 |
| Storage | 39 |

**35. General.**—*a. Historical sketch.*—European history contains references to black powder as early as A. D. 1250. Roger Bacon in 1264 performed the first recorded experiments with this material, and shortly after this time it was introduced as a propelling charge for the fourteenth century bombard. Authorities differ upon the subject of the origin of black powder. It has been attributed severally to the Chinese, Arabs, and Hindus. It is certain that the alchemists of medieval days were familiar to a certain extent with the properties of the mixture of saltpeter, sulphur, and charcoal. Certain authorities regard Berchtold Schwarz as the inventor. To him at any rate belongs the credit of being the first (A. D. 1313) recorded user of this material in the propelling of stones from a gun. Powder was first used in a meal state. Later camphor was added to prevent crumbling. Graining or granulating is first recorded in 1425, resulting in a stronger and more uniform powder. Classification of the grains by screening is reported by the French in 1525.

*b. Use.*—(1) Black powder gradually replaced all other devices as a propellant, until 1870 it was practically the only propellant used. Its present military use is practically confined to—

(*a*) Ignition charges.

(*b*) Base charge or expelling charge for shrapnel shell.

(*c*) Manufacture of primers and fuses.

(*d*) Saluting and blank-fire charges.

(*e*) Time-train rings and combination fuses.

(2) It is thus seen that in its former function as a propellant, black powder has been superseded almost entirely, having been replaced by smokeless powder. Among some of the factors which may be mentioned as responsible for effecting this change are—

(*a*) Large quantity of solid residue after ignition of charge.

(*b*) Volume of smoke caused by presence of a large quantity of noncombustible material.

(c) Relatively great speed of erosion of the gun barrel due to high temperature of combustion.

(d) Rapid deterioration when exposed to atmospheric conditions due to its hygroscopic nature.

**36. Manufacture.**—*a. General.*—(1) *Precautions.*—The manufacture of black powder is not technically complicated, but owing to its sensitivity unusual precautions must be observed in its manufacture.

(2) *Composition.*—Black powder is a mechanical or physical mixture of potassium nitrate or sodium nitrate, charcoal, and sulphur in the approximate proportions of 75, 15, and 10, varying percentages being used with varying effects. Potassium nitrate is used in manufacture of the powder for all military uses except charges for saluting ammunition. The commercial blasting powder made with sodium nitrate is now used for saluting charges. The saltpeter and sulphur is of a very high grade commercial quality and is practically free from chlorides and chlorates. Purification of saltpeter is obtained by means of repeated recrystallization, the formation of large crystals being prevented by continuous agitation of the saltpeter liquor. Charcoal is obtained from burning of peeled willow, alder, or suitable hardwood. Depending upon the use to which the particular grade is to be put, the percentage composition of the finished material is altered as necessity demands. It has been found, for instance, that by increasing the percentage of saltpeter the rate of burning is increased; by increasing the percentage of charcoal the rate of burning is decreased. Extensive incorporation improves the quality and uniformity.

*b. Process.*—(1) The sulphur and charcoal in the proportions specified are pulverized in a ball mill which consists of a revolving steel cylinder in which iron or steel balls do the crushing or grinding. This pulverized material is mixed either with pulverized saltpeter or stirred into a saturated solution of saltpeter, depending on the plant equipment. The three methods of mixing are—

(a) French, which is rarely used in this country. The pulverized saltpeter, charcoal, and sulphur are mixed and incorporated in a ball mill in which the revolving cylinder is of hardwood and part of the balls are lead composition and part lignumvitae.

(b) Dry mixing, in which the ingredients are blended by hand or by mechanical devices. In each of the above methods a small quantity of water is added.

(c) Wet mixing, in which the pulverized sulphur and charcoal are stirred into a saturated solution of saltpeter at a temperature of about 130° C. (265° F.). The mass is then spread on a floor to cool, after which it is ready for incorporation. The lumps formed in the cooling are easily broken.

(2) After mixing by either of the above methods, the material is spread on the bed of the wheel mills in quantities of 300 pounds per wheel mill. The wheels, weighing 8 tons each, rotate on the material for 3 hours at 10 rotations per minute. Edge runners keep the material worked toward the center of the tread of the wheels. Wheel cake or clinker formed during this operation is crushed or broken before pressing.

(3) In order to obtain uniform ballistic results, it is necessary that the powder be of uniform density before granulation. The horizontal hydraulic press has been found to be the best type for this operation. The press plates, usually of aluminum, are so placed as to give press cake approximating 3/4 inch in thickness and about 24 inches square. The effective pressure on the press cake is about 1,200 pounds per square inch.

(4) The press cake is cracked or granulated in the corning mill by feeding the cake between crusher rolls. Mechanically operated shaking screens separate the dust and coarse grains from the finished grain, the coarser lumps passing through successive crushing rolls, four sets of crushing rolls being the usual number per mill. The operation is considered as the most hazardous of the various operations in the manufacture of black powder. Many devices have been employed to reduce the loss of property and life in the corning mill to a minimum.

c. *Finishing.*—Rounding or polishing the grain is accomplished by tumbling in a revolving wooden cylinder. Drying may be done in the same cylinder by forcing a current of warm air through the cylinder while the powder is being polished, or the powder may be removed from the cylinder and dried in stationary wooden trays. To glaze the grains a small quantity of pulverized graphite is added to the powder while the powder is hot from the tumbling process and the process continued for about half an hour. The drying and glazing process, when carried out on the single operation plan, requires approximately 8 hours.

37. **Packing.**—Before packing, the powder is rescreened and separated into grades according to specification requirements. Containers for black powder are made of soft steel and average about 9 inches in diameter by 11 inches high, capacity 25 pounds, painted black, stenciled to show grades, lot number, maker, and contract number.

**38. Inspection.**—*a. Grades.*—(1) The various grades of black powder specified by U. S. Army specifications are as follows for potassium nitrate powder, using U. S. standard sieves:

| Designation | Wire screen | | | |
|---|---|---|---|---|
| | Passer | | Duster | |
| | Series number | Opening, inches | Series number | Opening, inches |
| Army black powder: | | | | |
| Grade A: | | | | |
| No. 1 | 4 | 0. 187 | 8 | 0. 0937 |
| No. 3 | 12 | . 0661 | 16 | . 0469 |
| No. 4 | 16 | . 0469 | 40 | . 0165 |
| No. 5 | 40 | . 0165 | 100 | . 0059 |
| No. 6 | 100 | . 0059 | 140 | . 0041 |
| Fuze powder | 140 | . 0041 | | |

(2) Sodium nitrate powders have the following granulations:

(*a*) Class A:

Through a No. 12 sieve, 100 percent.

Through a No. 16 sieve, not less than 45 percent.

On a No. 40 sieve, not less than 99 percent.

(*b*) Class B:

Through a No. 4 sieve, 100 percent.

On a No. 16 sieve, not less than 99 percent.

(3) In addition, Class A powder is used in pellet form, one or two pellets constituting a saluting charge. The above powders are intended for use as follows:

| Designation | Uses |
|---|---|
| Army black powder: | |
| Grade A: | |
| No. 1 | All igniting charges and the M1, M1B1, M21, and M22 primers; it may be used for saluting charges. |
| No. 3 | Special uses. |
| No. 4 | Base charges for shrapnel; base charges for fuzes; friction primers, M1914, obturating friction primers; M23 and M25 primers; smoke-puff charges; bursting charges for practice bombs; practice loaded projectiles; and certain subcaliber shell. |
| No. 5 | Pellets for primers and fuzes. |
| No. 6 | Do. |
| Fuze powder | Loading time-train rings. |
| Sodium nitrate powder: | |
| Class A | Saluting charges. |
| Class B | Practice bombs. |

*b. Tests.*—Methods prescribed for testing are as follows:

(1) *Samples.*—About 50 grams of the original sample are crushed in small portions in a porcelain mortar and passed through a 60-mesh sieve. All precautions are taken to avoid unnecessary exposure of the sample to air during this treatment. If each portion is placed in a stoppered bottle as soon as sifted, there is no appreciable change in hygroscopic moisture content. The powdered sample is well mixed before its analysis is begun.

(2) *Moisture.*—About 2 to 3 grams of the ground sample to pass at least 60-mesh fineness are spread in a thin layer on a tared 3-inch watch glass, carefully weighed, and dried over sulphuric acid in a desiccator for 3 days or in a drying oven at a temperature of 60° to 70° C. to constant weight (about 2 hours). Cooled in desiccator and weighed. Loss of weight is calculated as percent moisture.

(3) *Potassium nitrate.*—Into a tared Gooch crucible provided with an asbestos mat a known weight, approximately 10 grams, of sample is weighed. By means of suction about 200 cc. of hot water in successive portions of 10 to 15 cc. each are drawn through the crucible. The final portions of water passing through the crucible are tested with an excess of strong sulphuric acid containing a few crystals of diphenylamine until there is no blue color reaction indicating the presence of nitrates. The crucible is dried for 1 hour at 70° C. and weighed. The percentage loss in weight minus the moisture content is considered as the potassium nitrate content. (It is recognized that this includes any water-soluble portion of the charcoal or sulphur.) To test purity of the nitrate, 1 cc. of nitric acid (1.42 sp. gr.) is added to the water extract and evaporated to dryness and dried at 150° C. The residue is mixed and 1 gram tested for nitrogen content in a nitrometer. The nitrogen content of the residue should be 13.84 percent ±0.03 percent.

(4) *Sulphur.*—The dried and weighed material left from the extraction with water consists of the sulphur and charcoal. The sulphur is determined by loss of weight on extraction with carbon disulphide in the Wiley extractor or other suitable extraction apparatus, drying the insoluble residue to constant weight at about 100° C.

Before drying this residue in a hot oven, the carbon disulphide should first be allowed to evaporate by placing the crucibles in a warm place away from any flame or other source of high temperature, as the vapors of carbon disulphide are very inflammable.

(5) *Charcoal.*—The residue left from extraction of the sulphur is the charcoal which is weighed direct as already noted.

(6) *Ash.*—The ash of the charcoal is determined by ignition of the insoluble residue over a Bunsen burner until all of the carbon

has been burned off, and weighing. The ash usually amounts to about 0.5 to 1 percent of the total powder. An unusually high value for ash may indicate incomplete extraction with water.

(7) *Specific gravity.*—A known weight of approximately 10 grams is placed in a strong 50-cc. specific gravity bottle with a perforated glass stopper. The bottle is filled ½ to ⅔ full with clean mercury, placed under vacuum, and the remaining space filled with mercury. The bottle containing the powder and mercury is weighed at 19° to 21° C. Actual weight of the bottle plus mercury plus powder subtracted from the gross weight of bottle full of mercury, plus the powder taken at 19° to 21° C. represents the weight of mercury displaced. This weight divided by the specific gravity of mercury at 19° to 21° C. (13.59) gives the weight of an equal volume of water. The weight of the powder used divided by this weight of water represents the specific gravity of the powder.

NOTE.—To displace the air from the specific gravity bottle, a piece of heavy rubber tubing about 2 feet long is attached to the bottle. The other end of the rubber tubing is attached to one leg of a Y-tube. The other leg of the tube is extended by means of a small piece of glass tubing and rubber tubing to dip into a vessel containing mercury. The stem of the Y is connected with the suction line. The rubber tube leading to the mercury vessel is closed by means of a pinch cock. The suction is applied, the specific gravity bottle evacuated, and the suction line closed by means of a pinch cock placed close to the specific gravity bottle. The pinch cock on the tubing leading to the mercury vessel is opened to allow the mercury to flow into the specific gravity bottle. This operation is repeated until the bottle is filled with mercury.

(8) *Granulation determination.*—A sample of about 100 grams of the powder is weighed out accurately, emptied into the passer screen, and shaken vigorously over a sheet of brown paper for exactly 1 minute. The powder which has passed through the screen is set aside. The material remaining in the sieve is emptied onto the sheet of brown paper, striking the screen sharply with the fingers to remove any adhering powder grains. The material so obtained is sifted again for exactly 1 minute, the sieve emptied, and any grains adhering to the mesh removed, after which the material is submitted to a third sifting. The material which has now failed to pass through the screen is collected, weighed to the nearest tenth of a gram, and the percentage of powder which failed to pass through the passer screen is calculated. All the material which has been used in the passer screen test is now emptied onto the duster screen and sifted three times as described above, collecting each time the material which passed through the screen. This material is collected, weighed, and the percentage of powder which passed through the duster screen calculated.

(9) *Moisture- and ash-free.*—Percentages on a moisture- and ash-free bases are calculated by dividing the percentages of potassium nitrate, sulphur, and carbon, respectively, by the remainder obtained by subtracting the sum.of the percentages of moisture and ash from the sum total of the percentages obtained for potassium nitrate, sulphur, carbon, moisture, and ash.

**39. Storage.**—*a. Safety precautions.*—(1) In consideration of storage of low explosives, of which black powder is an example, it must be remembered that these materials are particularly sensitive to flame or spark. The restrictions relative to carrying matches, cleanliness of magazine floors, smoking, and use of nonsparking tools in general should be rigidly enforced and carefully supervised.

(2) When working in magazines where black powder is stored it is advisable to wear safety shoes, the so-called "powder shoes".

(3) When it becomes necessary to open a box or container of black powder it should always be done with a wooden wedge and mallet, at least 100 feet from the nearest magazine, and in a place which is protected from dampness or direct sunlight. No metal tools of any description will be used.

(4) If it becomes necessary to repair a magazine, all explosives should be removed to a safe distance and the building washed before work is started.

*b. Magazines.*—Black powder should be stored preferably in a bullet-proof magazine. It should not be stored in the same building with dry picric acid, dynamite, or other high explosive. The kegs may be placed in the magazine either on their ends with bung down, or sides with seam down. In view of the fact that black powder has a tendency to absorb moisture which causes deterioration and seriously affects properties of the powder, it is important that the storage magazines are dry and well ventilated.

## MILITARY HIGH EXPLOSIVES

### Section I

### GENERAL

Paragraph

Requirements_____ 40

Manufacture _____ 41

**40. Requirements.**—When the entire field of high explosives is considered, the term "military high explosive" has a restricted application to a relatively small number of substances. In determining suitability of a high explosive for military use, careful consideration must be given to its various properties including—

*a.* Strength.

*b.* Sensitivity to shock or friction such as may occur in loading.

*c.* Ability to withstand shock of set-back in the gun.

*d.* Ability to withstand penetration by bullets in the case of drop bomb explosives.

*e.* Stability.

*f.* Hygroscopicity.

*g.* Action on metals, etc.

These various requirements, together with questions of availability of raw materials, have excluded many high explosives which may be used successfully for commercial purposes.

**41. Manufacture.**—In the case of some of the explosives discussed in this manual, details of manufacture are not described as such data are regarded by manufacturers as confidential,

### Section II

### TRINITROTOLUENE (TNT)

Paragraph

General _____ 42

Properties_____ 43

Manufacture_____ 44

Nitration _____ 45

Purification_____ 46

Use _____ 47

Inspection _____ 48

Storage_____ 49

**42. General.**—*a. Uses.*—Although trinitrotoluene was known as early as 1863, it was not suggested as an explosive until about 1890, and its importance from a military standpoint dates from 1904. Since that time it has appeared as the principal constituent of many explosives, and has been used by itself under such various names as triton, trotyl, tolite, trilite, trinol, tritolo, etc. It is commonly known in this country by the abbreviation TNT. The term trinitrotoluol, which is more generally used than trinitrotoluene, is less correct from the chemical point of view than the latter.

*b. Characteristics.*—The importance of this explosive is based upon its relative safety in manufacture, loading, transportation, and storage, on the fact that it is not hygroscopic, on the lack of any tendency to form unstable compounds with metals, and upon its powerful, brisant, explosive properties.

**43. Properties.**—*a. Color and solubility.*—TNT usually resembles in appearance light brown sugar, although in different grades of refinement or purity its color and appearance vary. When pure it is a crystalline powder of very pale straw color. It dissolves readily in ether, acetone, alcohol, and various other solvents, but it is practically insoluble in water.

*b. Classification.*—TNT is classified in U. S. Army Specifications into two grades designated as grade I, with a setting point of 80.2° C. minimum, and grade II, with a setting point of 76.0° C. minimum. Grade II is obtained directly by the nitrating process as described below, while grade I must be prepared by recrystallization or by special chemical treatment of grade II material.

*c. Safety precaution.*—Both grades of TNT are slightly toxic, and it is necessary that proper precaution be taken by those engaged in its manufacture or handling to avoid inhaling the vapors or dust from the molten or crystalline material. Good ventilation in manufacturing or shell loading plants is highly essential, and personal cleanliness should be enforced. All clothing should be changed upon the beginning and completion of work.

*d. Stability.*—TNT is one of the most stable of high explosives, and when properly purified may be stored over long periods of time without alteration. It is quite insensitive to blows or friction but can be detonated by severe impact between metal surfaces. When ignited by flame it burns rapidly without explosion. Burning or rapid heating of large quantities especially in closed vessels may, however, cause violent detonation. It should therefore be melted in equipment so arranged that the maximum temperature of the melting unit cannot exceed 105° C.

*e. Chemical action.*—While TNT has no tendency to form compounds with metals thereby producing sensitive salts, it will react with alkalies such as sodium hydroxide or sodium carbonate to form unstable sodium salts which are quite sensitive. For this reason the use of alkalies in purification of TNT is not permissible.

*f. Detonation.*—(1) *Detonator.*—TNT in crystalline form detonates readily under the influence of a No. 6 detonator (containing 1 gram of mercury fulminate). When compressed to a high density it requires a No. 8 detonator (containing 2 grams of mercury fulminate), and when cast it is necessary to employ a booster charge of pressed tetryl, or an explosive of similar high brisance, to insure complete detonation.

(2) *Rate.*—TNT may be classed as a "quick acting" explosive. It detonates at a rate varying from about 5,200 meters per second for loosely compressed material to nearly 7,000 meters per second for material cast or compressed to its maximum density.

*g. Decomposition.*—(1) *Formulas.*—The decomposition of TNT on explosion may be regarded as occurring according to one or both of the following reactions:

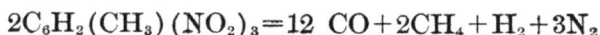

$$2C_6H_2(CH_3)(NO_2)_3 = 12\ CO + 2CH_4 + H_2 + 3N_2$$

or

$$2C_6H_2(CH_3)(NO_2)_3 = 12\ CO + 5H_2 + 3N_2 + 2C.$$

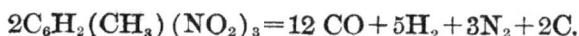

(2) *Oxygen compensation mixtures.*—The deficiency in oxygen as indicated by both of these reactions is always apparent from the black smoke produced by the explosion of TNT. This deficiency of oxygen may be compensated for by addition of such substances as ammonium nitrate or sodium nitrate in various proportions, the resulting mixtures being designated as amatol and sodatol, respectively.

**44. Manufacture.**—Manufacture of TNT involves the following processes:

*a.* Nitration of—

(1) Toluene to mononitrotoluene.

(2) Mononitrotoluene to dinitrotoluene.

(3) Dinitrotoluene to trinitrotoluene.

*b.* Washing finished product until free of acid.

*c.* Purification by remelting and chemical treatment or recrystallization.

*d.* Granulation, screening, and drying.

**45. Nitration.**—*a. Processes.*—The process for nitration of toluene with a mixture of nitric and sulphuric acids may be carried out in various ways, for example by the—

(1) One-stage process, where a large excess of a strong mixed acid is used and the temperature gradually raised, with the result that

trinitrotoluene is produced in the one process without transfer or separation of spent acid from intermediate products.

(2) Two-stage process, where either mono- or dinitrotoluene is produced in the first stage and trinitrotoluene in the second.

(3) Three-stage process, where by use of three different acid mixtures and different conditions of temperature, etc., there are successively produced mono-, di-, and trinitrotoluene.

*b. Three-stage process.*—The one-stage and two-stage processes have been superseded by the more practical and more economical three-stage process. A general description of the three-stage process follows:

(1) *First.*—The normal charge used in the manufacture is 1,300 pounds of toluene. The first step in the nitration is accomplished by running into the nitrator approximately 1,200 pounds of mono spent acid. The purpose of adding the spent acid is to provide a very weak charge as a bottom layer so as to prevent stripping the nitrating acid of nitric acid and also to raise the toluene level so that it will come in contact with the cooling coils. If this spent acid is not added, stripping of the nitrating acid is likely to occur which results in a charred mononitrotoluene. The amount of acid used in the mononitration is based on a nitric ratio of 1 part of toluene to .9 parts of nitric. The composition of the mixed acid is 76 percent sulphuric, 23 percent nitric, approximately. The agitation used during this nitration should be slow enough to prevent mixing of the toluene and the acid; that is, a separating line between these two components should be maintained throughout the nitration. The acid is added through a spider distributor and the temperature maintained at 50° C. for the first 2,000 pounds, between 50 and 55° C. for the next 4,000 pounds, and at 55° C. for the balance of the charges. The nitration is accomplished by the acid dropping through the toluene. After all the acid has been added, the charge is cooked for 10 minutes, cooled to 45° C., allowed to settle for 15 minutes, and the acid charge run off. The acid used in this nitration where a plant is in continuous operation is made up by fortifying the spent acid from the dinitration.

(2) *Second.*—This stage consists in nitrating the mononitrotoluene to dinitrotoluene. The mononitrotoluene obtained in the first stage is blown from the mononitrating house to the di-tri-nitrating house and placed in the di-tri-nitrator. The charge is first cooled to 45° C. The mixed acid used in this nitration is usually a fortified acid made by adding nitric to a spent acid from a previous trinitra-

tion.  The strength of the acid approximates that used in the mononitration, the nitric ratio being the same as for the mononitration.
The acid is added to the mononitrotoluene and the temperature
allowed to increase by 3-degree steps until it has reached a temperature of 80° to 83° C.  It is held at this point for the completion of
the nitration.  After all acid has been added, the charge is cooked
for 30 minutes and cooled to 60° C., settled for 30 minutes, and the
spent acid discharged.  This spent acid is forwarded to the fortifying house for the addition of nitric acid so that it may be used
in the next mononitration.

(3) *Third.*—In this stage, the dinitrotoluene is nitrated to trinitrotoluene.  It is this stage of manufacture that offers the most difficulty
and extremely strong acids are required to obtain a complete nitration.  To do this it is necessary to employ an anhydrous acid.
Approximately 3,500 pounds of fuming sulphuric acid is added to
the di-oil.  This acid is added gradually, the temperature being
allowed to rise in 3-degree steps until a temperature of 80° C. has
been reached.  As soon as the fuming sulphuric has been added the
mixed acid is started.  The mixed acid has a composition of 57
percent nitric and 41 percent sulphuric, approximately.  The nitrating temperature in this stage is 85° C. at the start with a gradual
rise in 3-degree steps until it reaches 104° C.  From this point the
nitration is continued until a test of the oil shows it has a freezing
point of 72° C. or higher.  Normally it requires 3 hours of nitration
after all the acid is in to obtain this setting point.  After this, the
charge is cooled to 100° C. and allowed to settle for 30 minutes,
after which the spent acid is sent to the fortifiers and the tri-oil to
the neutralizing house.

*c. Yield.*—(1) Humphrey (see par. 89) states that contrary to
usual belief, yield of TNT from the di or second nitration at a given
temperature is not the function of the water content of the mixture
(except that too strong an acid tends to oxidize the material and in
this manner lowers the percentage of yield), but is rather dependent
upon the proper low temperature during nitration.

(2) The mononitration yields a product containing a mixture of
about 4 percent of the meta nitrotoluene in addition to the ortho and
para isomers.  The subsequent nitration changes the meta mononitrotoluene chiefly into the beta and gamma trinitrotoluenes, which
differ from the alpha form in chemical properties and are regarded
as impurities.  Small amounts of other isomers of trinitrotoluene
have also been identified in the product of the complete nitration of
toluene.  Depending upon the completeness with which the last nitra-

tion is performed there may be either a large amount of dinitro-toluene present if improperly carried out, or, if correctly done, a relatively small amount.

(3) In addition to these impurities, there may also be such bodies as tetranitromethane which possesses the undesirable property of lowering the solidification point of the pure alpha TNT. If the nitration has been properly carried to completion, there should not be present more than 4 percent beta and gamma TNT. This condi-tion is not usually attained under manufacturing conditions and it is therefore necessary to recrystallize the TNT or purify it by other means in order that the impurities may be eliminated, and a product of the required solidification point for grade I, TNT (80.2° C.), obtained.

**46. Purification.**—*a. Process and equipment.*—The crude trini-trotoluene, which, due to the temperature of nitration, is in the form of an oil, is run from the nitrator into neutralizing tubs which have the shape of a cone at the bottom. At the apex of the cone a gate-way valve for regular discharge from the tub is provided. Steam coils for heating and air coils for agitation are both provided. Wash water is drawn off by means of suction through a suitable pipe which reaches the tub near the top and extends along the side wall to about 2 feet from the bottom. A small quantity of sodium sulphite can be used to assist in the purification at this point, although it is not necessary to do so. Washing is carried on until no test for acidity is shown by the use of litmus paper. The neutral TNT in the form of oil is now pelleted by running into cold water for transportation to the graining house, or can be transported in the molten condition to suitable storage tanks through heated pipe lines. If pelleted, these pellets are transported to storage tanks as above mentioned, and again melted before running into the crystallizing kettles. The storage tanks are kept at an approximate temperature of 95° C., and are provided with a gateway screw valve from which the molten charge is drawn off into the graining kettles. These kettles are made of cast iron in one piece, and the junction of the bottom and the side walls is rounded so that plows can scrape the TNT loose from the sides. The lower part of the kettle is fitted with a jacket into which steam or cold water may be discharged. As the plows are started, the charge cools down and the crystals begin to form on the sides which increase until the whole mass becomes plastic. During the operation all moisture is driven off and the TNT produced is in a fine crystalline condition. The TNT produced is usually better than grade II; that is, it has a melting point above 76° C. If it is desirable to obtain TNT of grade I, recrystallization from either sulphuric acid or other suitable solvent, or a treatment with sodium sulphite may be made. A brief description of each is given below.

b. *Crystallization from sulphuric acid.*—The fine crystals produced in the graining kettles are dissolved in hot sulphuric acid, usually weight for weight, and cooled. The purified crystals thus settling out are washed free from acid and regrained to such degree of fineness as to pass U. S. Army specifications. The crude material held in sulphuric acid is accumulated until such time as the amount warrants separate purification.

c. *Sulphite treatment.*—The sodium sulphite treatment may be applied by taking the fine crystals from the graining kettles, and placing them in bins or cars which are equipped with a Filtros bottom. These bins or cars are given one hot-water washing, then four washings with the 5-percent solution of sodium sulphite, then one warm-water washing followed by sufficient cold-water washings to remove the last traces of the red color which is formed in the treatment. The purified crystals thus obtained can be dried, sieved, and packed, or regrained, as may be necessary to meet specifications.

**47. Use.**—a. *Bursting charge.*—(1) Grade I TNT is slightly more expensive than grade II because it requires the additional purification. Grade I is used as the bursting charge for high-explosive shell, either alone or mixed with an equal weight of ammonium nitrate to form 50/50 amatol (the TNT in either case being melted so that the shell is filled by a casting or pouring process). Grade II is used only in 80/20 amatol, where it is mixed in the molten state with four times its weight of ammonium nitrate and filled into high-explosive shell by hand stemming or by means of a screw filling machine.

(2) A charge of about 1¼ pounds of cast TNT in a 75-mm high-explosive shell weighing about 10 pounds breaks up the shell into approximately 400 fragments retained on a 4-mesh screen.

(3) Other military uses for TNT are as a bursting charge for rifle grenades, airplane drop bombs, naval submarine mines, depth bombs, and as a constituent of propellent powder. In airplane bombs it has the disadvantage that penetration of the bomb by a rifle bullet may cause an explosion of the charge. This is also true of amatol, which is used extensively in drop bombs.

b. *Demolitions.*—TNT is also used for military purposes in demolition work on bridges, railroads, etc., and for land mines placed under enemy trenches or fortifications. For demolition work carried on by the Corps of Engineers, the TNT is made up in the form of small, highly compressed blocks inclosed in a fiber container which protects them from crumbling in handling and renders them waterproof.

c. *Blasting work.*—TNT has been demonstrated to be suitable for all kinds of blasting work where 40 percent dynamite is used and to give practically equal effects. It is well adapted for "adobe" shooting or "mud capping," terms applied to breaking up large rocks or bowlders by means of a charge of high explosive placed on the rock and confined only by means of a shovelful of mud or wet earth thrown over it. Only quick-acting explosives can be successfully used for such work. Even in drill holes containing water, TNT gives excellent results because of the fact that it is insoluble in water. However, its use for blasting has been negligible because of the fact that it is expensive as compared with commercial dynamites.

d. *Detonating fuse.*—"Cordeau Bickford," a trade designation for detonating fuse, consists of a flexible lead tube, smaller in diameter than a lead pencil, filled with TNT. It is quite entensively used in certain blasting operations, especially for insuring complete detonation of large charges of dynamite. The detonating fuse, being passed through the entire length of the charge and detonated at its external end by means of an ordinary blasting cap, transmits its high rate of detonation to the entire charge of dynamite.

**48. Inspection.**—a. *Specifications.*—Chemical and physical requirements prescribed by U. S. Army specifications for the different grades of TNT are as follows:

| | Grade I | Grade II |
|---|---|---|
| Solidification point, not less than. | 80.2° C. | 76.0° C. |
| Insoluble matter, not more than (percent). | 0.10. | 0.10. |
| Moisture, not more than (percent). | 0.1. | 0.1. |
| Acidity as $H_2SO_4$, not more than (percent). | 0.01. | 0.01. |
| Color | Light yellow. | Light yellow. |
| Granulation, not less than 95 percent shall pass through. | No. 14 U. S. standard sieve, opening 0.055 inch. | No. 14 U. S. standard sieve, opening 0.055 inch. |

It will be noted that the specifications for the two grades vary only in solidification point.

b. *Tests.*—The most important test in connection with the inspection of TNT is the determination of its solidification point or "setting point." This temperature serves as an indication of the purity of the explosive inasmuch as the presence of moisture, lower nitrated products, objectionable amounts of isomers, and other impurities all tend to lower the solidification point. However, in order to insure proper degree of purity, additional determinations of insoluble matter, moisture, and acidity are required by U. S. Army specifications. Prescribed methods of conducting these tests are as follows:

(1) *Solidification point.*—(*a*) *Apparatus.*—The apparatus used consists of the following parts: A test tube 1 inch in diameter and 6 inches long is fitted through a cork into a second test tube 1½ inches in diameter and 7 inches long, which in turn is set into a large-mouthed liter bottle. Into the inner tube is fitted a cork stopper through which are three openings. One is in the center for the standard thermometer, which should be graduated in $\frac{1}{10}°$ C. One is immediately at the side of the center hole and is for a small thermometer which is passed just through the stopper and which reading is taken as the average temperature of the exposed stem of the standard thermometer in making the stem correction. The third hole in the stopper is a small V-shaped opening at the side, through which passes a wire whose lower end is bent in a loop at right angles to the axis of the tube and which is used as a stirrer.

(*b*) *Method.*—A 50-gram sample of TNT is placed in the inner tube and melted in an oven, maintained at 95 to 100° C, the inner tube being separated from the rest of the apparatus for this purpose. When the TNT has completely liquefied, the tube is replaced in the apparatus, the standard thermometer placed so that the bulb is approximately in the center of the molten TNT, and the small side thermometer put in place. The stirrer should already be in the molten TNT. Stirring is continued vigorously as the temperature falls, and the thermometer must be watched very carefully. When a point is reached where the temperature begins to rise owing to the heat of crystallization, readings should be recorded about every 15 seconds until the maximum temperature is noted. This temperature usually remains constant for several minutes until crystallization is complete, and observation should be continued until it is certain that the maximum temperature has been reached. This takes from 5 to 10 minutes after beginning of crystallization. This maximum temperature with the correction for emergent thread is taken as the solidification point of the sample.

(2) *Insoluble matter.*—A known weight, approximately 10 grams, is boiled with 150 cc. of 95-percent ethyl alcohol or benzene, filtered

while hot through a tared Gooch and washed with hot additional solvent. After drying to constant weight at 100 cc., the crucible is cooled and weighed.

(3) *Moisture.*—A known weight, approximately 5 grams, is exposed in a desiccator over sulphuric acid in a watch glass for 48 hours.

(4) *Acidity.*—A known weight, approximately 10 grams of the sample, is melted and shaken with 100 cc. of neutral boiling water and allowed to cool. The sample is then remelted and again extracted with 50 cc. of neutral boiling water. The total water extract is cooled and titrated with N/10 sodium or potassium hydroxide, using phenolphthalein as an indicator. The results are calculated as percent sulphuric acid in the original sample.

(5) *Granulation.*—A weighed portion of approximately 100 grams and a small crucible lid, a 25-cent piece, or a similar object are placed on the specified sieve and shaken for 3 minutes. The portion retained on the sieve is weighed and the percentage passing through the sieve calculated.

**49. Storage.**—*a. Magazines.*—(1) *Construction.*—The type of magazine best designed for storage of TNT is approximately 26 feet wide and 42 feet long and when grouped together in a magazine area they are usually spaced 400 or 800 feet apart. They are constructed with concrete foundation walls or piers, hollow tile or brick walls, and wood floors. The flat roof supported on wooden roof trusses is of gypsum blocks or slabs covered with a fire-resistant built-up roofing. There are ventilators on the roof and in the foundation walls below the floor. The openings in the foundation walls are always well-screened or baffled to prevent entrance of sparks. The limiting floor load is 300 pounds per square foot. The bulletproof explosives magazine is similar in construction to the magazine described above except that the hollow tile walls are filled with sand or are made of materials which will stop rifle bullets.

(2) *Capacity.*—These magazines were originally designed for storage of 250,000 pounds of explosives, but with ample aisle space for inspection and shipping, and piles of convenient height, the amount is usually limited to approximately 100,000 pounds.

(3) *Fire.*—If a fire occurs in a magazine in which TNT is stored in wooden boxes, the explosive will usually burn quietly, but may possibly detonate. If the fire has gained considerable headway before it is discovered, no attempt should be made to fight the fire.

*b. Safety precautions.*—(1) It is desirable but not required that safety shoes be worn when handling, storing, and shipping TNT in

93

boxes.   Safety shoes should be worn in repacking rooms or buildings, or whenever loose TNT is being handled.

(2) Boxes should be opened and repaired with nonsparking tools.

(3) A container should never be opened in a magazine in which explosives or ammunition are stored.

SECTION III

AMMONIUM PICRATE (EXPLOSIVE D)

|                                                                 | Paragraph |
|-----------------------------------------------------------------|-----------|
| General                                                         | 50        |
| Properties                                                      | 51        |
| Manufacture                                                     | 52        |
| Use                                                             | 53        |
| Inspection                                                      | 54        |
| Storage                                                         | 55        |

**50. General.**—*a. Historical sketch.*—The use of ammonium picrate as an explosive was patented by Nobel in 1888 (Mosenthal, Jour. Soc. Chem. Ind., Vol. 18, p. 447, May, 1899), although even prior to that time Brugere made use of a mixture of ammonium picrate and sodium nitrate as a propellant explosive.

*b. Characteristics.*—The importance of ammonium picrate as a military explosive is due entirely to its marked insensitiveness to shock and friction, which makes it well suited for use as a bursting charge in armor-piercing projectiles.   From the standpoint of explosive strength, however, this explosive is inferior to TNT.

**51. Properties.**—*a. Color and solubility.*—Ammonium picrate is soluble in water, crystallizing from its solution in orange-yellow needles darker in color than picric acid.   It resembles picric acid in its bitter taste and property of dyeing the skin, clothing, etc., of those engaged in its manufacture or handling.

*b. Hygroscopicity.*—It has a much greater tendency to absorb moisture than has picric acid, samples having been found to absorb over 5 percent by weight of water during storage for 1 month in an atmosphere saturated with moisture.

*c. Chemical action.*—Like picric acid, ammonium picrate can react with metals to form metallic picrates, but it reacts with much less readiness than picric acid; in fact, when dry its action is almost negligible.   Wet ammonium picrate reacts slowly, especially with copper or lead, to form picrates which are particularly sensitive and dangerous.

*d. Heat action.*—Ammonium picrate does not melt on heating, but explodes when heated to a temperature of about 300° C. Small traces of metallic picrates may however lower this ignition temperature appreciably.

*e. Sensitiveness.*—Ammonium picrate is the least sensitive of all military explosives used as the bursting charge for shell. Its insensitiveness to shock accounts for it being given preference over TNT or amatol as the bursting charge for armor-piercing, base-fuzed shell. It is also more insensitive to detonation by means of mercury fulminate than is TNT. At a pressure of about 12,000 pounds per square inch the two explosives have the same densities, about 1.48.

*f. Toxicity.*—Like TNT and picric acid, ammonium picrate liberates free carbon on explosion, giving a black smoke. The products of explosion, although more disagreeable in odor, are less poisonous than those from TNT and picric acid in that they contain less carbon monoxide.

**52. Manufacture.**—*a. Process.*—The manufacture of ammonium picrate consists in the main of a simple neutralization of picric acid by means of ammonia either alone or in combination with ammonium carbonate. This process is not attended with any serious manufacturing difficulties or dangers. provided one excludes the possibility of leaking ammonia pipes.

*b. Method.*—Details of manufacture are as follows: Approximately 300 pounds of picric acid are mixed with 500 gallons of water at room temperature and then slowly heated by direct steam. As the mixture warms, aqua ammonia is added at the bottom of the tank until neutralization is completed. In some factories it was the practice to add a faint excess, thus insuring complete neutralization of all the picric acid, this condition being evidenced by the formation of a reddish colored crystalline mass of ammonium picrate. U. S. Army Specifications permit a maximum of .025 acidity or alkalinity. When this stage has been reached the resulting material is dropped into tanks for crystallization. These tanks are so equipped that a continual agitation of their contents can be maintained by air with the object of accelerating the crystallizing of the ammonium picrate during the cooling. When the mass has cooled to about 25° C. the crystals are separated from the mother liquor by filtering or draining. From the crystallizing tank the ammonium picrate is taken to the dry house where it is subjected to a temperature of about 45° C. for 8 hours in drying bins which are so constructed that warm air circulates constantly through the mass. Finally the dried material is screened by means of a rotating screen and sent directly to the packing room. The finished product is then packed in 50-pound boxes lined with waterproof paper and sent to storage.

*c. Reworking ammonium picrate.*—This operation consists in redissolving impure or waste ammonium picrate in water, removing the impurities by filtration, then heating the solution by steam coils until it has been evaporated sufficiently to produce crystallization. From here on the reworking operations are exactly the same as those followed out in the manufacture of the new material.

**53. Use.**—As has been mentioned, ammonium picrate is used as the bursting charge for armor-piercing shell on account of its insensitiveness to shock which permits the shell to pass through the armor without exploding. Owing to the fact that it cannot be melted without decomposing, it must be loaded into the shell by pressing. The interior of the shell is covered with a suitable nonmetallic paint or varnish. It has no commercial use as an explosive, although it enters into the composition of numerous patented blasting explosives which have not been used to any great extent.

**54. Inspection.**—*a. Specifications.*—U. S. Army Specifications prescribe the following requirements for ammonium picrate:

(1) Ammoniacal nitrogen, not less than 5.64 percent.

(2) Moisture, not more than 0.2 percent.

(3) Solubility, not more than 0.2 percent insoluble.

(4) Ash, not more than 0.2 percent.

(5) Acidity or alkalinity, not more than 0.025 percent.

(6) Color, yellow to red.

(7) Granulation:

(*a*) Through No. 14 U. S. standard sieve, 99.5 percent minimum.

(*b*) Through No. 100 U. S. standard sieve, 20 percent maximum.

*b. Tests.*—The following tests and determinations are made on ammonium picrate to determine its suitability for military use:

(1) *Ammoniacal nitrogen.*—A known weight, approximately 1 gram of the ammonium picrate to be analyzed, is placed in a 500-cc. Kjeldahl flask. The flask is equipped with a two-hole rubber stopper which carries an exit tube leading away to a bottle containing N/10 sulphuric acid, and an ingress tube reaching to its bottom, through which air that has already been dried and freed from ammonia by passage through concentrated sulphuric acid may be bubbled. Twenty cc. of water is introduced into the flask, 12 cc. of 5-percent sodium carbonate solution added, the flask set in a boiling water bath and ammonia-free air bubbled through until contents of the flask have

been evaporated to dryness. The ammonia is absorbed by bubbling the air through 50 cc. of N/10 sulphuric acid, a bulb full of very small holes such as may be made conveniently with a hot platinum wire being used for the purpose. To deal with the possibility of splashing of the sulphuric acid, the exit tube from the bottle is equipped with a trap. The excess sulphuric acid is titrated with N/10 sodium hydroxide, using methyl red or sodium alizarin sulphonate as an indicator, the amount which has been consumed is noted, and the ammoniacal nitrogen in the sample is calculated as follows:

$$\text{Percentage of ammoniacal nitrogen} = \frac{1.401 \ (AB - CD)}{E}$$

where A=number of cc. of sulphuric acid solution in bottle.
B=normality of sulphuric acid solution.
C=number of cc. of sodium hydroxide solution used.
D=normality of sodium hydroxide solution.
E=weight of sample.

(2) *Moisture.*—A sample of about 5 grams of the ammonium picrate is accurately weighed in a previously tared wide-mouthed weighing bottle at least 1½ inches in diameter and dried for 2 hours or to constant weight in a drying oven at 100° C. The loss of weight is calculated as percentage of moisture in the original sample.

(3) *Insoluble material.*—A known weight, approximately 10 grams, is dissolved in 150 cc. of hot distilled water by boiling for 10 minutes. The solution is filtered through a tared Gooch filter, the insoluble residue washed thoroughly with hot water, and dried for 1 hour at 100° C.

(4) *Mineral matter (ash).*—A known weight, approximately 2 grams, is wetted with molten paraffin in a tared crucible and carefully burned until all carbonaceous residue has been eliminated. It is cooled in a desiccator and weighed.

(5) *Acidity or alkalinity.*—A representative sample of 5 grams of the ammonium picrate is ground in a porcelain mortar with 50 cc. of water at room temperature, and the supernatant liquid poured through a folded filter, the filtrate being caught in a 500-cc. Erlenmeyer flask. This process is repeated until all of the ammonium picrate is brought into solution and the total volume of the filtrate is 250 cc. Three drops of sodium alizarin sulphonate or a 1-percent alcohol solution of methyl red indicator are added. The solution is acid as shown by either of the indicators assuming a yellow color. If the solution is acid, it is titrated with approximately 0.1 N sodium

hydroxide solution and the percentage of picric acid in the sample calculated as follows:

$$\text{Percentage of picric acid} = \frac{22.905 \text{ AB}}{C}$$

where A=number of cc. of sodium hydroxide solution used.
   B=normality of sodium hydroxide solution.
   C=weight of sample.

If the solution is alkaline as shown by the indicator assuming a purple or red color, it is titrated with approximately 0.1 N sulphuric or hydrochloric acid. The percentage of free ammonia in the sample is calculated as follows:

$$\text{Percentage of free ammonia} = \frac{1.7034 \text{ AB}}{C}$$

where A=number of cc. of acid solution used.
   B=normality of acid solution.
   C=weight of sample.

(6) *Granulation.*—A No. 14 U. S. standard sieve is fitted on a No. 100 U. S. standard sieve and a receiving pan attached to the bottom sieve. A weighed portion of 100 grams of the sample and two metal washers are placed on the upper sieve, covered, and shaken 3 minutes. The material retained on the No. 14 sieve and that passing through the No. 100 sieve are weighed and calculated each in terms of percentage.

**55. Storage.**—*a. Regulations.*—Storage of ammonium picrate is governed by the same regulations as are applicable for the storage of TNT both as to type of magazine and rules for handling, and special regulations governing this particular explosive are not necessary.

*b. Special precautions.*—(1) Ammonium picrate which has been pressed at a shell-loading plant and removed from a shell is very much more sensitive to shock or blow than new material, and there are cases on record where serious accidents have happened in the loading of shell with ammonium picrate so treated. If it becomes necessary to store this material, special precautions should be observed to protect it against shock or fire, and it preferably should be stored in a building by itself.

(2) Although less sensitive than TNT ammonium picrate can be exploded by severe shock or friction, is highly inflammable, and when heated to a high temperature may detonate. It is therefore necessary that it be treated with proper care as a high explosive.

*c. Magazines.*—Since it absorbs moisture it should be stored in dry magazines and protected from dampness. Moisture, however, has no effect on ammonium picrate except to reduce its explosive strength and its sensitiveness to detonation.

*d. Containers.*—Ammonium picrate is always stored in wooden containers because of the possibility of its forming metallic picrates in contact with metals, especially when moist.

SECTION IV

## PICRIC ACID

| | Paragraph |
|---|---|
| General | 56 |
| Properties | 57 |
| Manufacture | 58 |
| Use | 59 |
| Inspection | 60 |
| Storage | 61 |

**56. General.**—Picric acid or trinitrophenol was first adopted as a military high explosive by the French Government in 1886 under the name of melinite, and has since been used to a greater or less extent by almost all countries with or without addition of various materials intended to reduce its melting point. The British explosive designated as lyddite and the Japanese explosive schimose are both cast picric acid, and various names are given to other shell explosives the chief component of which is picric acid.

**57. Properties.**—*a. Color and solubility.*—Picric acid is a lemon-yellow, crystalline solid, only slightly soluble in cold water but soluble in alcohol, benzene, and other organic solvents. A very small amount is, however, sufficient to color a large volume of water a distinct yellow color. It likewise stains the skin of workmen, colors clothing, hair, and everything else with which it comes in contact, and has an exceedingly persistent, disagreeable, bitter taste. Its property of coloring is utilized in the dye industry, and in fact, picric acid was long known as a dyestuff before its explosive nature was discovered. It has no tendency to absorb moisture from the air.

*b. Heat action.*—Picric acid melts at a temperature of about 122° C. when pure, and is usually required for explosive use to have a melting (or solidifying) point of at least 120° C.

*c. Chemical action.*—Being an acid, it has the property of combining with ammonia and alkalies and with many of the metals, forming salts which are called picrates. Some of the picrates are much more sensitive than picric acid itself, and it is therefore necessary that formation of these picrates be avoided by keeping picric acid from direct contact with those metals with which it readily reacts.

*d. Precautions.*—Picric acid is not as toxic as TNT and the chief danger in connection with its use is probably the fumes given off from the molten explosive in loading shell. While practically no trouble from poisoning results in manufacture or handling of picric acid, care must be taken, however, to avoid breathing the large amounts of picric acid dust that may arise in screening or packing the dry material.

*e. Stability.*—Picric acid is entirely stable. It has no tendency to decompose at any temperatures which it might meet in storage. On sudden heating at temperatures much above its melting point (122° C.) it may explode, although many cases are noted where considerable quantities of picric acid have burned without explosion. Presence of any trace of explosive that will detonate more readily such as metallic picrates may cause sudden detonation of burning picric acid.

*f. Detonation.*—It has about the same sensitivity to shock or friction as TNT and is somewhat more readily detonated by means of a detonator. Picric acid is one of the most powerful of military explosives. Its high strength or concussive effect is due to its high rate of detonation which, for the cast or highly compressed explosive, is about 7,000 meters per second, slightly greater than that of TNT under the most favorable conditions. By both the Trauzl lead block test and the ballistic pendulum test, picric acid shows appreciably greater strength than TNT, being exceeded only by tetryl and TNA. The results of these methods of testing are confirmed by actual fragmentation tests of high-explosive shell where it is found that a larger number of shell fragments are produced from picric acid than from TNT at equal loading densities.

**58. Manufacture.**—*a. Material.*—The raw material from which picric acid is derived is benzene (often called benzol). This substance must not be confused with benzine which is essentially gasoline obtained by distillation of petroleum. Benzene is an inflammable liquid obtained as a byproduct in manufacture of coke, by recovery from illuminating gas, or by "cracking" oils at high temperatures.

*b. Processes.*—Picric acid may be manufactured from benzene by two distinct processes designated respectively as the phenol and the chlorbenzene process.

(1) *Phenol.*—(*a*) *Benzene conversion.*—Practically all of the picric acid produced in this country during the World War was made from phenol (carbolic acid). Phenol is prepared from benzene as a

raw material by first treating pure benzene with strong sulphuric acid and heating the mixture in jacketed iron kettles provided with agitation at a temperature of about 90° C. for several hours. The resulting benzene sulphonate is usually treated with lime which converts it to calcium benzene sulphonate, which in turn is converted to sodium benzene sulphonate by means of sodium carbonate (soda ash). The sodium benzene sulphonate is dried and heated in fusion kettles with caustic soda which converts it into sodium phenate. The fusion mixture is dissolved in water and treated with either carbon dioxide or sulphuric acid which causes the phenol to separate out as a distinct layer. This layer is drawn off and distilled in order to separate the pure phenol from water and other impurities. Pure phenol is a white crystalline solid which melts at about 40° C.

(*b*) *Phenol conversion.*—For conversion to picric acid the phenol is melted into large jacketed iron kettles and treated with sulphuric acid of about 93 percent strength, the mixture heated with stirring at a temperature of about 95° C. from 4 to 6 hours. The resulting phenol sulphonic acid is diluted with water and treated in a large acidproof, brick-lined nitrator with 42° Baumé nitric acid (about 70 percent). The reaction generates heat and the mixing is therefore carried on very slowly, the maximum temperature being about 110° C. After cooling the mixture, the crystallized picric acid is separated from the spent acid on a vacuum filter, washed with water, and dried.

(2) *Chlorbenzene.*—Although this process has been quite extensively used abroad, its use in this country until recently has been rather limited. Briefly, the process involves first, treatment of benzene with gaseous chlorine whereby monochlorbenzene results. This product is purified by distillation and then nitrated with a mixture of nitric acid and sulphuric acids to give dinitrochlorbenzene. The latter on treatment with lime or soda loses its chlorine and becomes calcium or sodium dinitrophenolate, which on acidifying is converted to dinitrophenol. The dinitrophenol is readily nitrated to picric acid (trinitrophenol) by means of nitric and sulphuric acids.

**59. Use.**—*a. General.*—The fact already noted that picric acid combines readily with some metals to form picrates which are unduly sensitive to friction, shock, or heat has been detrimental to the use of picric acid for military purposes in spite of the fact that it is a stronger explosive than TNT. When a nonmetallic lining is used for the shell cavity as for instance, certain lacquers, varnishes, or paints, danger of formation of these salts is obviated to a great degree. Introduction of TNT as a military explosive has resulted in gradual abandonment of picric acid by practically every country except France where it was largely used during the World War. In the United States it is used for conversion into "Explosive D" or ammonium picrate which is used in base-fuzed shell for seacoast cannon. Picric acid has also found use as a booster explosive and even as a substitute for part of the mercury fulminate charge in detonators.

*b. Mixtures.*—Picric acid has been used extensively in the form of mixtures with other nitrocompounds. Such mixtures having a lower melting point than picric acid can be melted and cast at temperatures below 100° C. The mixtures are more generally practicable because of the hazard involved in melting picric acid at the relatively high temperature required. Some of the compounds which have been used with picric acid are trinitrotoluene, trinitrocresol, trinitrobenzene, and the di and mono nitro derivatives of phenol, cresol, and naphthalene. Little, if any, change in brisance results from the addition of the trinitro compounds, but the addition of the mono and dinitro compounds causes a reduction in brisance in proportion to the amount added.

**60. Inspection.**—*a. Specifications.*—Chemical requirements prescribed for picric acid by U. S. Army Specifications are as follows:

(1) It must have a solidification point of not less than 120° C.

(2) It must contain—

(*a*) Moisture, not more than 0.2 percent if purchased dry, and not more than 22 percent if purchased wet.

(*b*) Sulphuric acid, not more than 0.1 percent, both free and combined.

(*c*) Nitric acid, no free.

(*d*) Ash, not more than 0.2 percent.

(*e*) Material insoluble in water, not more than 0.2 percent.

(*f*) Lead, not more than 0.0004 percent.

(3) It must be of a white to yellow color.

(4) Not less than 99.5 percent shall pass a No. 14 U. S. standard sieve.

*b. Tests.*—Methods prescribed for testing are as follows:

(1) *Solidification point.*—A sample of the picric acid to be used for this test must be dried to constant weight at a temperature not exceeding 50° C. The apparatus used consists of the following parts: A test tube 1 inch in diameter and 6 inches long is fitted through a cork into a second test tube 1½ inches in diameter and 7 inches long, which in turn is set into a large-mouthed liter bottle. Into the inner tube is fitted a cork stopper through which are three openings. One is in the center for the standard thermometer which should be graduated in $\frac{1}{10}$° C. One is immediately at the side of the center hole

and is for a small thermometer which is passed just through the stopper and which reading is taken as the average temperature of the exposed stem of the standard thermometer in making the stem correction. The third hole in the stopper is a small V-shaped opening at the side through which passes a wire whose lower end is bent in a loop at right angles to the axis of the tube and which is used as a stirrer. The inner test tube is removed and charged with approximately 50 grams of the sample. It is than placed in an oven at a temperature of 130° C. until the picric acid has attained the temperature of the bath throughout. The tube is then assembled in the apparatus for cooling, the standard thermometer graduated in $\frac{1}{10}$° immersed in the picric acid with its bulb in the center of the molten mass, and stirring continued vigorously as the temperature falls. The temperatures of both thermometers should be recorded every 15 seconds in order to note the maximum temperature reached on the slight rise of temperature which results during crystallization. This maximum temperature corrected for emergent mercury column is taken as the solidification point.

(2) *Moisture.*—A sample of about 5 grams of the picric acid is accurately weighed in a previously tared wide-mouthed weighing bottle at least $1\frac{1}{2}$ inches in diameter, and dried for 5 hours or to constant weight in a drying oven at 70° C. The loss of weight is calculated as percentage of moisture in the original sample.

(3) *Sulphuric acid.*—A known weight of picric acid, approximately 10 grams, is dissolved in 250 cc. boiling distilled water, filtered and washed with 25 cc. of hot distilled water, acidulated with hydrochloric acid, and the solution heated. A slight excess of hot solution of barium chloride is then added with constant stirring, the precipitate allowed to settle, and filtered while hot on a tared Gooch crucible. The latter is washed thoroughly with hot water, dried for 3 hours at 100° C., and the weight of $BaSO_4$ calculated as $H_2SO_4$ in the original sample.

(4) *Nitric acid.*—A water solution of picric acid is tested with a solution of diphenylamine in concentrated sulphuric acid. No coloration should result.

(5) *Ash.*—A known weight, approximately 5 grams, is moistened with strong sulphuric acid in a tared crucible and carefully burned until all carbonaceous residue has been eliminated. To compensate for reduction of metallic salts, a few drops of nitric acid and sulphuric acid are added, carefully evaporated, the crucible again ignited, cooled in a desiccator, and weighed.

(6) *Insoluble material.*—10 grams of the sample is dissolved in 150 cc. of boiling water, boiling continued for 10 minutes. The solution is

filtered while hot through a tared Gooch crucible which is washed thoroughly with hot water, and dried for 2 hours at 100° C.

(7) *Lead.*—A known weight, approximately 300 grams of the picric acid, is placed in a 2-liter flask and allowed to soak in 100 cc. of a hot saturated solution of barium hydroxide in 65 percent alcohol. The flask is well shaken, 1,400 cc. of 95 percent alcohol added, and the whole allowed to digest at a temperature below the boiling point of alcohol until all the picric acid has been dissolved with the exception of small particles of insoluble matter. The solution is shaken thoroughly and allowed to stand in the cold until most of the picric acid has crystallized out, then filtered. It is not necessary to disturb the crystalline picric acid at the bottom of the flask as only 500 cc. of the solution is used for completion of the tests and this amount can be decanted. To 500 cc. of this filtered solution which represents 100 grams of picric acid, four or five drops of nitric acid and 10 cc. of a 1 percent mercuric chloride solution are added and a slow stream of hydrogen sulphide passed through this solution for 15 minutes. After allowing to settle 20 minutes, the solution is filtered and the precipitate washed with alcohol saturated with hydrogen sulphide, the filter paper dried and ignited in a porcelain crucible; 9 cc. of nitric acid, sp. gr. of 1.42, is added and the solution warmed on a hot plate. Enough warm water is then added to make up the volume to 50 cc. The solution is electrolized with a current of 0.4 ampere and 2½ volts, temperature 65° C. using a tared platinum anode. After 1 hour, the electrode is washed by replacing the beaker with another one full of distilled water without interrupting the current. The tared anode is dried and weighed. The weight of lead peroxide found by difference multiplied by 0.8661 gives the percent of lead.

(8) *Granulation.*—A weighed portion of 50 grams of the sample is placed on a No. 14 U. S. standard sieve to which a bottom pan has been attached. Two metal washers are placed on the sieve and shaken for a maximum of 3 minutes or until no more material passes through the sieve. Any material remaining on the sieve is weighed and the percentage passing through the sieve calculated.

**61. Storage.**—Rules governing storage of dry picric acid are the same as for TNT. Dimension of magazines should not exceed 42 by 26 feet. It is necessary that all dust accumulating from dry picric acid should be carefully removed from any point in or around the buildings, conveyors, or cars. Although dust originating from this source is not as dangerous as that from black powder, it is nevertheless a matter of record that serious explosions have been caused from this source. Safety shoes must be worn in every instance where picric acid is being handled.

SECTION V

## NITROSTARCH EXPLOSIVES

|  | Paragraph |
|---|---|
| General | 62 |
| Manufacture | 63 |
| Properties | 64 |
| Use | 65 |
| Storage | 66 |
| Inspection | 67 |

**62. General.**—*a.* During the World War certain explosives having nitrostarch as a base were used under the designations "Trojan grenade explosive," "Trojan trench mortar shell explosive," and "Grenite." These explosives were frequently referred to as "nitrostarch," but it should be noted that pure nitrostarch was not used alone as a military explosive, the nearest approach to it for military purposes being grenite, which was about 95 percent nitrostarch, the balance being a binding material added for the purpose of granulating. The two Trojan explosives which were practically identical in composition contained approximately 25 percent nitrostarch with ammonium nitrate, sodium nitrate, and small amounts of materials added for the purpose of stabilizing, reducing sensitiveness and hygroscopicity, and neutralizing any possible acidity of other ingredients.

*b.* These nitrostarch explosives were used for the reason that at the time the United States entered the war a decided shortage of TNT was indicated and investigation showed nitrostarch explosives to be entirely suitable for trench warfare purposes and to offer the advantages of low cost and ample supply of raw materials, etc.

**63. Manufacture.**—*a.* *Process.*—(1) *Starch conversion.*—Nitrostarch is prepared by treating starch with a mixture of nitric and sulphuric acids. It can be prepared from any variety of starch, but it is claimed that a cassava or tapioca starch gives a slightly more stable product than cornstarch. The starch is first freed from impurities such as fats, oils, and water-soluble matter, then carefully dried at low temperatures, and screened. It is fed slowly into the acid mixture in a nitrator provided with suitable agitation and cooling surface. This treatment converts the starch into starch nitrate (commonly but incorrectly referred to as nitrostarch), without any change in appearance, but with a decided change in chemical properties.

(2) *Starch nitrate treatment.*—The nitrated product is separated from the excess of spent nitrating acid, drowned in water, washed thoroughly to remove all traces of free acid, then separated from the water in filters or centrifugal wringers, and finally spread on trays to

dry in suitable dry houses heated with air at a temperature of 35°
to 40° C.

*b. Drying:*—The drying operation, especially handling the warm,
dry product, is the only really dangerous operation connected with
manufacture, the dry nitrostarch being highly inflammable, capable
of being ignited by the slightest spark such as might result from a
static charge,and when once ignited, burning with explosive violence.

*c. Mixing.*—Mixing dry nitrostarch with the "dope" materials,
as the inert ingredients of such explosive mixtures are frequently
called, is a simple operation carried out in large revolving mixing
barrels.    All of the dope materials must first be ground to the proper
degree of fineness and dried to the proper moisture content so that
the moisture content of the finished explosive will not be in excess
of the prescribed amount.    Granular nitrostarch explosives such as
Grenite are usually prepared by spraying the dry material with a
solution of the binding material while the mixture is being agitated
in a revolving mixer.    The resulting granules are dried and screened
to proper size.

**64. Properties.**—*a. Color and solubility.*—(1) *Nitrostarch.*—Nitrostarch is a white, finely divided material similar in appearance
to ordinary powdered starch.    When observed under the microscope
there is no appreciable difference between nitrated and unnitrated
starch until the granules are treated with iodine which colors the
unnitrated starch blue but does not affect the nitrated product.
Nitrostarch is insoluble in water and does not gelatinize or form a
paste when heated with water, thereby differing from starch.    The
grade of nitrostarch ordinarily employed contains from 12.50 to
12.75 percent nitrogen; that prescribed for military purposes contains at least 12.80 percent.    All nitrostarch is readily soluble in
acetone, solubility in ether-alcohol in general increasing as the nitrogen content decreases.    It has no great tendency to absorb moisture
from the atmosphere beyond the amount of 1 to 2 percent.

(2) *Trojan explosive.*—Trojan grenade or trench mortar shell explosive differed greatly in appearance and in certain of its properties
from straight nitrostarch, being of grayish-black color and of about
the consistency of ordinary brown sugar, having a slightly damp
feel and tendency to pack under compression due to the small amount
of mineral oil contained as an ingredient.    This oil, besides decreasing the sensitiveness of the explosive to ignition and to shock or
friction, helped to reduce its attraction for moisture, the mixture of
ammonium nitrate and sodium nitrate which it contained being very
hygroscopic.    In spite of this coating of oil the Trojan explosive

when spread out in a thin layer in a damp atmosphere rapidly absorbed moisture to such extent that it became decidedly wet. Under ordinary working conditions therefore great care was taken in loading this explosive to avoid absorption of an undesirable amount of moisture.

(3) *Grenite.*—Grenite, which was almost entirely pure nitrostarch with addition of a small amount of oil and a binding material, differed greatly in appearance from Trojan explosive, being in the form of small, white, hard granules which flowed freely without sticking together. Since it contained no ammonium nitrate or other hygroscopic materials, Grenite had no particular tendency to absorb moisture even in damp atmospheres.

*b. Sensitivity.*—(1) Pure dry nitrostarch is more sensitive to impact than TNT but less sensitive than dry guncotton or nitroglycerin. As mentioned above, it is highly inflammable and readily ignited by the slightest spark such as may result from friction, and like black powder burns with explosive violence. It is readily detonated by by a mercury fulminate detonator.

(2) Trojan explosive and Grenite were both much less sensitive than straight nitrostarch, being required to pass the pendulum friction test of the United States Bureau of Mines and the rifle bullet test when packed in pasteboard containers. In heavy metal containers these explosives frequently ignited and burned when penetrated by a rifle bullet, and in rare instances exploded under this test. Trojan explosive was especially insensitive to ignition, being rather difficult to ignite with the flame of a match when spread out unconfined. When once ignited, however, especially in any quantity, it burned freely with a light-colored smoke.

*c. Detonation.*—Nitrostarch explosives were readily detonated by mercury fulminate detonators, a No. 6 detonator containing 1 gram of fulminate composition, producing complete detonation unless the explosive had been rendered unduly insensitive by absorption of excessive moisture or by other cause.

*d. Stability.*—Early attempts to manufacture nitrostarch resulted in production of material which was unstable, and numerous statements found in literature of explosives refer to nitrostarch as being unsatisfactory for use as an explosive because of sensitivity and instability. However, manufacturers in this country succeeded in placing on the market nitrostarch explosives which proved highly satisfactory in these respects and found considerable application as blasting explosives. Developments led to a product which met requirements prescribed for military explosives. However, the Trojan explosive if allowed to absorb undue quantities of moisture, especially in a warm atmosphere, tended to deteriorate, being quite similar to nitrocellulose in this respect.

**65. Use.**—*a. Trojan explosive.*—The Trojan nitrostarch explosive was used as the bursting charge for hand grenades, rifle grenades, and trench mortar shell. It was well adapted to such purposes but was not considered for use as a bursting charge for high-explosive gun shell. Its physical consistency was such that it was loaded into grenades through the small filling hole by means of vibrating machines, the explosive being "jarred" into the grenade through small funnel openings. Trench mortar shell were loaded by hand-stemming.

*b. Grenite.*—Grenite was used only for grenades and was considered too sensitive for use as a trench mortar shell explosive. Being granular and "free-running" it was readily loaded into the grenades through funnel openings, no attempt being made to pack it to a high density.

*c. Nitrostarch.*—(1) Nitrostarch has been considered for the manufacture of smokeless propellent powder and numerous attempts have been made to develop a satisfactory powder of this type, but the problem cannot as yet be considered solved.

(2) Nitrostarch explosives similar to Trojan grenade explosive have been used for a considerable number of years as blasting explosives for use in mining, quarrying, and other engineering operations, and have met with considerable success as substitutes for the more expensive nitroglycerin explosives.

(3) There has recently been adopted, after thorough investigation, a nitrostarch demolition explosive as a substitute for TNT. This explosive is somewhat similar to that used during the World War but the formula has been modified by raising the nitrostarch content and the replacement of the ammonium nitrate with barium nitrate. It can be consolidated into blocks in the same manner as TNT, and in comparison tests it has been found that the TNT formula for computing small charges are directly applicable to the nitrostarch demolition explosive.

**66. Storage.**—Storage of nitrostarch explosives in general is mainly a fire risk, that is, the danger accompanying storage is more one of fire than of explosion. However, burning may proceed at such rate as to be almost explosive in nature, and the fact that nitrostarch can be exploded by impact should not be overlooked.

*a. Magazines.*—Magazines should be kept at as low temperatures as possible in order to avoid as much as possible the tendency of nitrostarch to undergo decomposition on heating. A reasonably dry atmosphere in magazines is also essential for the Trojan explosive.

This explosive was not suitable for storage in bulk in wooden containers because of its hygroscopicity. Even when loaded into grenades it tended to absorb moisture. Long contact of the explosive with the metal parts of the grenade, either iron, brass, or copper, resulted in corrosion.

*b. Handling.*—There is no danger of poisoning of any kind connected with the handling of nitrostarch explosives.

**67. Inspection.**—*a. Specifications.*—(1) The chemical composition of Trojan explosive as used was as follows:

|  | Not less than— | Not more than— |
|---|---|---|
|  | Percent | Percent |
| Nitrostarch | 23. 0 | 27. 0 |
| Ammonium nitrate | 31. 0 | 35. 0 |
| Sodium nitrate | 36. 0 | 40. 0 |
| Charcoal | 1. 5 | 2. 5 |
| Heavy hydrocarbons | . 5 | 1. 5 |
| Antiacid | . 5 | 1. 5 |
| Diphenylamine | . 2 | . 4 |
| Moisture | | 1. 2 |

(2) The chemical composition of grenite is prescribed as follows:

|  | Not less than— | Not more than— |
|---|---|---|
|  | Percent | Percent |
| Nitrostarch | 95. 5 | 98. 25 |
| Petroleum oil | . 75 | 2. 00 |
| Gum arabic | . 75 | 2. 00 |
| Moisture | | 1. 00 |

*b. Tests.*—(1) *Trojan explosive*—The following methods for analysis of Trojan explosive were prescribed:

(*a*) *Moisture.*—Approximately 5 grams of the sample, accurately weighed out, are spread evenly on a 90-mm. watch glass (3½-inch diameter) and placed in a desiccator over concentrated sulphuric acid. Loss in weight after 48 hours is taken as moisture. As an alternative method, a vacuum desiccator may be used with sulphuric acid (sp. gr. 1.84) as a desiccating agent and employing a vacuum of at least 700 mm. of mercury. After 24 hours the vacuum is slowly relieved and the loss in weight taken as moisture.

(*b*) *Ether extract.*—Approximately 10 grams of the sample are accurately weighed out and placed in a porous crucible (Gooch crucible with thin asbestos mat, or an alundum filtering crucible) and extracted with pure petroleum ether of 0.640 to 0.660 specific gravity.

After complete extraction the crucible and contents are dried by means of a stream of dry air until complete removal of the petroleum ether, after which the crucible is placed in a steam oven and dried to constant weight at approximately 70° C. The difference in weight between the original weight of the sample after deducting weight of moisture and the weight after extraction is taken as the heavy hydrocarbon oil present, together with the diphenylamine. The diphenylamine in this mixture may be determined by means of the Dumas method for determining nitrogen.

(c) *Water extract.*—The material in the crucible after removal of the heavy oil consists of nitrostarch, ammonium nitrate, sodium nitrate, charcoal, and sodium bicarbonate. By treatment with warm distilled water the ammonium nitrate, sodium nitrate, and sodium bicarbonate are removed, and the material in the crucible after drying at 80° C. for several hours consists of nitrostarch and charcoal. The loss in weight in the water extraction is determined and also the weight of the crucible plus nitrostarch and charcoal. These two factors are then used in the subsequent calculations.

(d) *Sodium bicarbonate.*—The water extract is made up to a fixed volume. One portion is taken for the determination of the sodium bicarbonate present. This is determined by titration with N/10 sulphuric acid, using methyl orange as an indicator and the alkalinity so found is calculated to sodium bicarbonate.

(e) *Ammonium nitrate.*—At the option of the inspector, the percentage of ammonium nitrate is determined by taking an aliquot portion of the water extract, adding caustic soda until the solution is strongly alkaline, and then distilling in an apparatus as used for ammonia determinations and collecting the distillate in a known volume of standard sulphuric acid. The excess acid is titrated with standard alkali, methyl orange being used as an indicator, and the result is then calculated to ammonium nitrate.

(f) *Sodium nitrate.*—An aliquot part of the water extract is acidified with nitric acid and the solution evaporated to dryness in a platinum dish. It is then ignited at a low red heat over a suitable flame, using care to avoid loss of the contents. The weight is then taken and a correction made for the amount of sodium bicarbonate present and the results regarded as sodium nitrate present. Following this procedure, the ammonium nitrate would be taken by difference in order to avoid the determination of ammonia.

(g) *Charcoal.*—The residue in the crucible after the water extraction consists of nitrostarch and charcoal. This material is best extracted in a Wiley extractor with warm acetone until no further soluble material is obtained. The crucible is then dried in a stream of dry air and further dried for several hours at 100° C. The weight of the charcoal is taken as the increase in weight of the crucible over its original weight empty.

(*h*) *Nitrostarch.*—The difference between the sum of nitrostarch and charcoal content as determined in (*c*) above and the percentage of charcoal as found by (*g*) above represents the nitrostarch present.

(2) *Grenite.*—Analysis of Grenite is carried out in a similar manner, the ether extraction removing the oil, the water extraction dissolving the gum arabic and leaving the nitrostarch.

## Section VI

## TETRYL

Paragraph
General _____ 68
Manufacture_____ 69
Properties_____ 70
Use _____ 71
Storage and handling_____ 72
Inspection_____ 73

**68. General.**—The high explosive commonly known as tetryl is trinitrophenylmethylnitramine. It is a derivative of benzene and is therefore in the same class of aromatic nitro compounds as TNT. Tetryl was first synthesized by Mertens in 1877. It did not acquire prominence as a military explosive until the World War when it was used as a booster explosive.

**69. Manufacture.**—*a.* Although the explosive manufacturer starts with dimethylaniline as his raw material, the entire process beginning with benzene is as follows: Benzene is nitrated to nitrobenzene by means of a mixture of nitric and sulphuric acids and the resulting nitrobenzene reduced with iron filings and hydrochloric (muriatic) acid to aniline. Aniline is then combined with methyl alcohol (wood alcohol) by heating these ingredients under pressure in the presence of sulphuric acid or iodine, yielding dimethylaniline.

*b.* The dimethylaniline is an oily liquid of slightly lower specific gravity than water. Prior to nitrating it is dissolved in a large excess of approximately 96 percent sulphuric acid because if treated direct with mixed acid a very violent reaction results. This solution in sulphuric acid is now added to nitric acid or a mixture of nitric and sulphuric acids in a nitrator provided with means for cooling and agitation. The temperature of nitration is approximately 68° to 72° C.

*c.* The tetryl is separated from the acid mixture by filtration or by drowning in water and decanting the sour water. The tetryl is given short boiling treatments to reduce the total acidity to 0.5 percent or less. The excess water is removed by filtration and the crude tetryl thus obtained is purified by recrystallization from benzene, acetone, or nitric acid. In recrystallization conditions are so controlled that granulation of the finished product makes it free-flowing. This free-flowing property is required so as to allow the manufacture of tetryl pellets in automatic pelleting presses.

**70. Properties.**—*a. Chemical and physical.*—Tetryl is a fine crystalline powder of a yellow color, practically insoluble in water but soluble in acetone, benzene, and other solvents. It is readily recrystallized and can therefore be obtained in very pure condition if desired. It melts when pure between 129° and 130° C. Tetryl is poisonous when taken internally and precaution is necessary in its manufacture, especially regarding the dust encountered in handling and packing the dry material. It has a higher nitrogen content (24.4 percent) than any other military explosive. Tetryl is practically nonhygroscopic,. absorbing less than 0.1 percent moisture when stored for several days in a saturated atmosphere.

*b. Stability and sensitvity.*—Tetryl is stable at all temperatures which may be encountered in storage. When heated above its melting point it undergoes gradual decomposition and explodes when exposed to a temperature of 260° C. for 5 seconds. It is more sensitive to shock or friction than TNT, being of about the same order of sensitivity as picric acid. It is slightly more sensitive to detonation by means of mercury fulminate than TNT, and is readily exploded by penetration of a rifle bullet.

*c. Detonation.*—Tetryl has been found to have a rate of detonation somewhat higher than the maximum rate obtained with TNT (7,000 meters per second). Strength tests such as the Trauzl lead block test show tetryl to be stronger than any other military high explosive, the average expansion produced in the lead block for the more common military high explosives being as follows:

Tetryl, 320 cubic centimeters.

Picric acid, 300 cubic centimeters.

TNT, 260 cubic centimeters.

**71. Use.**—*a. Charges.*—(1) The high explosive strength and brisance of tetryl would seem to adapt it for use as a bursting charge, but its sensitivity to mechanical shock is such that if used as a shell filler it would not withstand shock of discharge of the gun. It is, however, sufficiently insensitive that when compressed into a booster it is perfectly safe. In this condition it is readily detonated by the detonator in the fuze of the shell, and the violence of its detonation insures a high order of detonation of the bursting charge.

(2) Tetryl has been adopted as a booster explosive. Formerly it was combined with TNT (grade I), the two explosives being usually loaded separately into the booster casing in the form of highly compressed pellets.

*b. Detonator.*—It is also used in detonators for both military and commercial purposes as a base charge, the tetryl being pressed into the bottom of the detonator shell and then covered with a small priming charge of mercury fulminate, lead azide, or other initiator.

**72. Storage and handling.**—The same precautions should be observed in storage and handling of tetryl as in the case of other sensitive high explosives. It should be kept dry because moisture interferes with its effectiveness. It must be properly protected from bullet fire in brick or hollow tile magazines with iron doors and window shutters. Detonators, blasting caps, fuzes, dynamite, etc., must not be stored with tetryl. Rubber-soled shoes should be worn in magazines and every precaution taken to prevent ignition or explosion from friction or blows due to rough handling.

**73. Inspection.**—*a. Specifications.*—U. S. Army Specifications require that tetryl will have—

(1) Melting point, not less than 128.5° C.

(2) Acidity, not more than 0.05 percent.

(3) Insoluble in benzene, not more than 0.20 percent.

(4) Moisture, not more than 0.10 percent.

(5) Color, light yellow or buff.

(6) Granulation:

(*a*) Through No. 12 U. S. standard sieve, 100 percent minimum.

(*b*) Through No. 16 U. S. standard sieve, 95 percent minimum.

(*c*) Through No. 100 U. S. standard sieve, 20 percent maximum.

(7) Sand test: 0.4 gram of tetryl primed with 0.24 gram mercury fulminate will crush not less than 45 grams standard Ottawa sand to pass a 30-mesh sieve on each of five trials.

*b. Tests.*—Prescribed methods of testing tetryl for acceptance are as follows:

(1) *Melting point.*—A portion of about 5 grams of the tetryl is ground in a mortar to pass a 100-mesh screen and this finely ground material used for the test after drying for 2 hours at 100° C. or in a sulphuric acid desiccator for 48 hours. The capillary tubes used must be of uniform external diameter of about 0.30 mm. to 0.80 mm. with light walls, and long enough to extend out of the bath of liquid used

for heating.  The thermometer must be accurately standardized and the mercury column completely immersed at the temperature of the observed melting point, or accurate corrections for emergent stem applied.  The capillary tube is filled to a depth of 3–4 mm. with the sample, compacted by tapping, and fastened to the thermometer with its bottom end in contact with the bulb of the thermometer.  The thermometer is then suspended in the bath with its bulb at least 1½ inches from the bottom of the bath.  The bath being provided with efficient agitation, its temperature is raised rapidly to about 120° C. and then very gradually so that the rise in temperature is about 1° in 5 minutes.  The point taken as the melting point is the temperature which is observed at the instant that the first meniscus of melted material appears across the capillary tube.

(2) *Insoluble matter.*—A known weight, approximately 5 grams, of the sample is dissolved in 75 cc. of benzene by heating to about 75° C. and filtered through a tared Gooch crucible.  The residue in the crucible is washed with 25 cc. of benzene, dried to constant weight at 100° C., and weighed.

(3) *Acidity.*—A weighed portion of approximately 5 grams of the sample is dissolved in 150 cc. of benzene.  The solution is transferred to a separatory funnel and shaken with 100 cc. of cold, recently boiled, distilled water.  The liquids are allowed to separate, the water drawn off, and the benzene solution washed with another 50 cc. of cold boiled water.  The combined water washes are titrated with approximately 0.1N sodium hydroxide solution, using phenolphthalein as indicator.  The acidity is calculated as percentage of sulphuric acid.

(4) *Moisture.*—A sample of about 5 grams of the tetryl is accurately weighed in a previously tared wide-mouthed weighing bottle at least 1½ inches in diameter, and dried for 2 hours in a drying oven at 100° C. or in a desiccator over sulphuric acid for 48 hours.  The loss of weight is calculated as percentage of moisture in the original sample.

(5) *Sand test.*—(a) *Loading the five caps.*—0.4 gram of tetryl weighed to the nearest milligram is placed in the empty shell of a commercial No. 6 blasting cap (composed of copper or gilding metal, and 1.46 inches long by 0.217-inch inside diameter) which is held in a loading block.  A plunger 0.20 inch in diameter is inserted in the shell and a pressure of approximately 3,000 pounds per square inch applied to the tetryl for 3 minutes.  0.24 gram of mercury fulminate weighed to the nearest milligram is placed in the shell and covered with a reinforcing cap (having a diameter of approximately 0.217 inch at the lower end and a hole of 0.11±0.03-inch diameter in the

top). The same pressure of approximately 3,000 pounds per square inch is applied for 1 minute.

The powder train in one end of a piece of miner's fuse 8 or 9 inches long is pricked with a pin, and a loaded cap crimped on to this pricked end of the fuse. Care should be taken to crimp near the mouth of the cap in order to avoid the danger of squeezing the fulminate. The cap should be held away from the body when the crimp is being made.

(b) *Method.*—80 grams$\pm$0.1 gram of standard Ottawa sand which have been previously sieved through a No. 20 U. S. standard screen and retained on a No. 30 U. S. standard screen are poured into the cavity of the sand test bomb and leveled by striking the bomb two or three times. The fuse is inserted through the hole in the cover of the bomb, and the cap lowered into the bomb cavity until the bottom touches the sand. One hundred and twenty grams$\pm$0.1 gram more of the sand (making a total of 200 grams) are then poured around the cap and the bomb tapped as before.

To avoid possible loss of sand caused by the explosion blowing the burned fuse out of the hole in the cover, a piece of rubber tubing about $\frac{1}{8}$ inch long and of such inner diameter that it fits the fuse snugly is slipped over the fuse and adjusted at a point on the fuse in such a manner that when the detonator is in position the rubber will be against the inner side of the bomb cover. The cover is then securely fastened to the bomb, taking care not to displace the cap in the sand. The fuse is lighted and after the explosion has taken place the sand is emptied onto a smooth (glazed) piece of paper, care being taken to remove completely any sand adhering to the sides of the bomb or to pieces of the detonator, shell, or burnt fuse. All of the sand is emptied onto the No. 30 U. S. standard sieve, and the amount which passes through after shaking for 3 minutes is weighed.

SECTION VII

MERCURY FULMINATE

|  | Paragraph |
|---|---|
| General | 74 |
| Manufacture | 75 |
| Properties | 76 |
| Use | 77 |
| Storage | 78 |
| Inspection | 79 |

**74. General.**—Mercury fulminate is one of the explosives used for bringing about detonation of high explosives. It detonates completely and with great violence on ignition by means of a flame such as the spit from a fuse or by means of an electrically heated wire. This fact, together with its property of initiating detonation of other explosives, makes it a most suitable detonator material.

75. **Manufacture.**—*a. Materials.*—Mercury fulminate is prepared, generally on a relatively small scale by the action of alcohol on mercury nitrate in nitric acid solution. The raw materials required are metallic mercury, nitric acid, and ethyl alcohol (common grain alcohol of 95 percent strength). All of these materials must be of high purity in order to produce a satisfactory product.

*b. Process.*—Process of manufacture is quite simple and may be carried out as follows:

(1) About 1 pound of pure mercury is weighed carefully, added to a weighed charge of from 8 to 10 pounds of strong nitric acid in a suitable bottle or acid pitcher, and allowed to stand until completely dissolved, giving a solution of mercury nitrate in the excess of nitric acid. A large number of such charges are usually prepared and allowed to stand over night until dissolved.

(2) The acid solution of mercury is then poured into about 8 to 10 pounds of 95 percent alcohol which has previously been measured into a large thin glass flask or balloon of about 10-gallon capacity supported in a suitable rack under an open shed or in the open air. A violent reaction results, usually within 2 or 3 minutes, the mixture in the balloons appearing to be boiling violently as a result of the evolution of great quantities of vapors and fumes. These vapors, at first white, become brownish red in color toward the end of the reaction as the heat generated drives off nitric acid. At this point a small amount of dilute alcohol is usually added to prevent excessive heating which would decompose the mercury fulminate produced. The reaction usually lasts about 1 hour. When fuming ceases, the liquid remaining in the balloon is found to contain the crystalline fulminate. In most plants the balloons are placed in troughs of water in order to control the temperature, and the necks of the balloons are connected with a suitable condenser system where the alcohol driven off in the fumes is recovered.

(3) After cooling, the charge in the balloons is dumped onto a cloth screen and washed with cold running water until all free acid is removed and the fine impurities in the form of "fulminate mud" washed away. The washed fulminate is then drained and packed in cloth bags which are usually stored in crocks of water in vaults, or in underground concrete tanks of water until required for use. For shipment the bags are packed in barrels of wet sawdust. When required for use, the fulminate is removed from the bags, the water

drained off, and the wet fulminate spread on cloth to dry in dry houses carefully regulated at a temperature of about 43° C. (110° F.). 1 pound of mercury produces approximately 1¼ pounds of dry mercury fulminate.

**76. Properties.**—*a. Color and solubility.*—Mercury fulminate is a heavy, crystalline solid, white when pure, but ordinarily of a faint brownish yellow or grayish tint. It has practically no tendency to absorb moisture from the atmosphere. It is only slightly soluble in water, 100 parts of water at 15.5° C. (60° F.) dissolving less than 0.01 part of fulminate, and may be kept in contact with water for long periods of time without undergoing change.

*b. Size of crystals.*—Size of the crystals of mercury fulminate is an important factor, since it has been determined that very finely divided fulminate consisting mostly of fragments of crystals and usually containing an excessive amount of impurities is less efficient in detonating value and strength than larger crystals. In specifying the size of crystals desired, however, consideration has been given to the possibilities of controlling this feature in manufacture and also to the fact that there is some reason to believe that very large crystals of fulminate are more sensitive to friction or shock than smaller ones. As indicated below, U. S. Army specifications for mercury fulminate prescribe definite limits for the size of the crystals.

*c. Impurities.*—Mercury fulminate is required by U. S. Army specifications to be at least 98 percent pure and the amounts of impurities which it may contain are strictly limited. The most objectionable impurities are—

(1) Free metallic mercury, for the reason that it readily attacks copper or brass with which it may be in contact when loaded into fuzes, detonators, or primers, causing the metal to become brittle.

(2) Acidity, which would cause deterioration of the explosive composition and corrosion of metal parts.

(3) Insoluble material such as sand and grit, which might cause explosion of the dry fulminate in loading operations.

If improperly manufactured or incompletely washed, the fulminate may also contain various compounds of mercury which might produce decomposition and would certainly diminish explosive efficiency.

*d. Stability.*—(1) Mercury fulminate has been kept for long periods both dry and wet, and is believed to undergo practically no change when properly manufactured and stored. However, when stored either wet or dry at tropical temperature gradual deterioration takes place. It has been found that when stored at 35° C. (95° F.) mercury fulminate deteriorated to the point of malfunctioning in about 3 years and at 50° C. (122° F.) it deteriorated to practically the same degree in 10 months. It is never stored in quantity in dry condition except when loaded into detonators, fuzes, or primers for the reason that when dry it is readily detonated by friction or shock. Whereas the great majority of high explosives will burn without detonating when ignited by a flame especially if a relatively small amount of the explosive is ignited, mercury fulminate is one of the so-called "primary" or "initiating" explosives which detonate completely on being heated to their ignition point by means of a flame or hot wire.

(2) The presence of even small amounts of moisture in mercury fulminate greatly reduces its efficiency, and as little as 1 percent is said to cause failure to detonate. However, fulminate completely saturated with water may be detonated by detonation of dry fulminate in contact with it.

*e. Sensitivity.*—(1) By usual methods of determining ignition temperature, mercury fulminate detonates at a temperature of about 180° C. (about 356° F.), but under varying conditions detonation may result at much lower temperatures. Sensitivity to shock is much greater at elevated temperatures than under storage conditions.

(2) When loaded into commercial detonators, mercury fulminate is usually compressed at pressures of about 3,000 pounds per square inch. In this condition its explosive properties are not appreciably different from those of loosely compressed material. At greater densities obtained by higher pressures, there is a gradual reduction in sensitivity, until at such extreme pressures as 25,000 to 30,000 pounds per square inch fulminate entirely loses its property of detonating when ignited and will only burn. In this condition it is referred to as "dead pressed." If, however, such highly pressed fulminate is initiated by loose fulminate or other initial detonating agent, it will detonate at even higher rates than are obtainable at low densities.

(3) Although fulminate can be pressed under very high pressures without explosion, the presence of any particles of sand or grit is very dangerous in any pressing operation. Presses for loading are always carefully protected by heavy barricades, and no one is permitted to be near the press during operation.

(4) The readiness with which dry mercury fulminate detonates from the effect of blows or friction is the chief reason for the fact that its transportation and storage in the dry state is not permitted. Tests with a special type of impact machine showed that mercury fulminate

detonated from the blow of the falling weight dropped from a height of only 2 centimeters (about 0.8 inch), while TNT in the same apparatus required a drop of about 120 centimeters (48 inches).

*f. Detonation.*—For a number of years mercury fulminate was considered to have special properties which made it an especially favorable initiating agent and numerous theories were advanced to account for its so-called "unique" properties. As a matter of fact, mercury fulminate has been used only because of its extreme sensitivity to flame or impact. In all other respects mercury fulminate is inferior to other high explosives such as TNT, tetryl, and picric acid as a detonating agent. For example, mercury fulminate has a rate of detonation of about 4,000 meters per second as compared with 6,800 meters per second for TNT under the same conditions. In the Trauzl lead block test, mercury fulminate produces an expansion of 213 cc. and TNT 260 cc. The trend in military and commercial detonators for the past several years has been gradual replacement of the major portion of the fulminate charge with some high explosive to increase efficiency of the detonator, the fulminate being used only as a cover charge to initiate detonation of the high explosive forming the base charge in the detonator.

**77. Use.**—Mercury fulminate is used only for the purpose of bringing about the detonation of other high explosives or the ignition of propellent explosives. In detonators for commercial or military use it may be used alone or mixed with from 10 to 20 percent of potassium chlorate. The usual grades of detonators contain from 15 to 30 grains of fulminate or its equivalent.

The ignition of propellant explosives, for example, smokeless or black powder in small arms cartridges, is effected by the flame from a primer or cap, the charge of which is usually a composition containing mercury fulminate mixed with other flame-producing materials such as potassium chlorate and antimony sulphide. The primer is initiated by impact of the firing pin.

**78. Storage.**—*a.* Mercury fulminate is always stored thoroughly saturated with water.

*b.* When left in the barrels during storage, regular inspection must be made to insure that the barrels are kept always full of water and are not leaking.

*c.* Fulminate must not be stored with any other explosives for the reason that explosion of even a relatively small amount of dry fulminate may cause detonation of the wet material, effect of which might be to detonate any other high explosives stored in the same building.

*d.* In case of breakage, or other cause by which wet ful minate may be spilled on the floor, it must not be allowed to dry out before cleaning up. Dry fulminate is very sensitive to friction and must be handled with extreme care. Spilled fulminate may be destroyed by washing floors, benches, etc., with a saturated solution of sodium thiosulphate.

**79. Inspection.**—*a. Specifications.*—Chemical and physical requirements for mercury fulminate as prescribed by U. S. Army specifications are—

(1) Fineness of such a degree that not more than 15 percent by weight will be retained on a No. 100 U. S. standard screen, and that not more than 75 percent will pass through a No. 200 U. S. standard screen.

(2) Acidity, none.

(3) Material insoluble in sodium thiosulphate, not more than 2 percent.

(4) Free mercury, not more than 1 percent.

(5) Chlorine, not more than 0.05 percent.

(6) Mercury fulminate, not less than 98 percent.

(7) Sand test: Not more than 0.27 gram will be required to detonate completely 0.4 gram of TNT having a melting point of at least 80.5° C., and of such granulation that it will completely pass through a No. 80 U. S. standard screen.

*b. Tests.*—Methods prescribed for testing are as follows:

(1) *Granulation.*—A known weight, approximately 10 grams of the dried fulminate obtained by drying at a temperature not exceeding 60° C to constant weight, is added to water and transferred to a 6-inch or some convenient size No. 100 U. S. standard sieve provided with a brass pan, and thoroughly shaken for 10 minutes under water. The residual fulminate is transferred from the No. 100 U. S. standard sieve to a tared filter paper, washed twice with alcohol and once with ether, and dried at 50° C. to constant weight. The fulminate which passes through the 100-mesh sieve is washed on a No. 200 U. S. standard sieve, and well shaken under water for 10 minutes. The fulminate passing through the sieve is transferred to a tared filter paper, washed twice with alcohol, once with ether, and dried in the same manner as the fulminate which remains on the 100-mesh sieve.

(2) *Acidity.*—A known weight, approximately 10 grams of the thoroughly dried material, is placed in a porcelain Gooch crucible provided with a filter paper disc in place of the customary asbestos mat and washed with two successive 25-cc. portions of boiled distilled

water. The filtrate so obtained should show no red tinge upon the addition of three drops of methyl orange solution prepared by dissolving 1 gram of methyl orange in water and making up to 1 liter.

(3) *Insoluble matter.*—A known weight of mercury fulminate, approximately 2 grams, is transferred to a 250-cc. beaker. One hundred and fifty cc. of freshly filtered 20 percent C. P. sodium thiosulphate solution at room temperature is added and the solution stirred for about 1 minute or until the mercury fulminate is apparently in solution. It is then filtered at once through a tared Gooch crucible. Any free mercury remaining in the beaker is completely washed into the crucible with distilled water. The crucible is washed with three or four 10-cc. portions of cold water to free it from sodium thiosulphate and dried at 70° C. to constant weight.

(4) *Free mercury.*—The residue in the Gooch crucible obtained from the insoluble determination is treated with 60 cc. of a sodium thiosulphate-potassium iodide solution containing 6 grams sodium thiosulphate and 3 grams potassium iodide dissolved in water and made up to 50 cc. The solution is decanted through the Gooch crucible containing the insoluble material and the crucible thoroughly washed with distilled water and dried at 80° to 90° C. for 2 hours and weighed. The residue remaining is taken as the mercury content and the percentage so determined.

(5) *Chlorides.*—A known weight, approximately 5 grams of the thoroughly dried material, is placed in a porcelain Gooch crucible having in its bottom a filter paper disk instead of an asbestos mat and washed with two successive 25-cc. portions of distilled water having a temperature between 90° and 100° C. To the filtrate, which is most conveniently caught in a test tube, three drops of pure nitric acid having a specific gravity of approximately 1.40, and 10 drops of a 10-percent solution of silver nitrate are added. No greater turbidity will appear than when a solution containing 0.0042 gram of pure sodium chloride dissolved in 50 cc. of distilled water is treated exactly as the filtrate from the sample of fulminate. This represents 0.05 percent of chlorine.

(6) *Mercury fulminate.*—Exactly 0.3 gram of the thoroughly dried material is placed in a wide-mouthed Erlenmeyer flask of approximately 250-cc. capacity, containing approximately 50 cc. distilled water. 30 cc. of a 20-percent sodium thiosulphate solution at room temperature is added quickly and the mixture shaken for exactly 1 minute and then titrated with standard 0.1N HCl solution, using three drops of methyl red as indicator.

It is important that the titration begin exactly 1 minute after addition of the thiosulphate. The bulk of the HCl should be added immediately, and the total time of titration should not exceed 1 minute. A blank determination should be run and the necessary correction made. The calculation is as follows:

$$\text{Percent mercury fulminate} = \frac{0.711565 \ (A - B) C}{D}$$

where A = cc. of HCl used.
     B = cc. required for blank.
     C = Normality factor for HCl.
     D = Weight of sample taken.

(7) *Sand test.*—(*a*) *Loading the five caps.*—0.4 gram TNT having a melting point of not less than 80.5° C. weighed to the nearest milligram is placed in the empty shell of a No. 6 blasting cap (composed of copper or gilding metal, 1.46 inches long by 0.211 inch inside diameter) which is held in a loading block. A plunger 0.20 inch in diameter is inserted in the shell and a pressure of approximately 3,000 pounds per square inch is applied to the TNT for 3 minutes. 0.27 gram of mercury fulminate weighed to the nearest milligram is placed in the shell and covered with a reinforcement cap (having a diameter of approximately 0.217 inch at the lower end and a hole of 0.11 ± 0.03-inch diameter in the top). The same pressure of approximately 3,000 pounds per square inch is applied for 3 minutes.

The powder train in one end of a piece of miner's fuse 8 or 9 inches long is pricked with a pin, and a loaded cap crimped on to this pricked end of the fuse. Care should be taken to crimp near the mouth of the cap in order to avoid danger of squeezing the fulminate. The cap should be held away from the body when the crimp is being made.

(*b*) *Method.*—Eighty ± 0.1 grams of standard Ottawa sand which have been previously sieved through a No. 20 Bureau of Standards sand screen and retained on a No. 30 Bureau of Standards sand screen (opening 0.0223 inch, wire diameter 0.011 inch) are poured into the cavity of the sand test bomb and leveled by striking the bomb two or three times (see fig. 29). The fuse is inserted through the hole in the cover of the bomb and the cap lowered into the bomb cavity until the bottom touches the sand. 120 ± 0.1 grams more of the sand (making a total of 200 grams) are then poured around the cap and the bomb tapped as before.

To avoid possible loss of sand caused by the explosion blowing the burned fuse out of the hole of the cover, a piece of rubber tubing

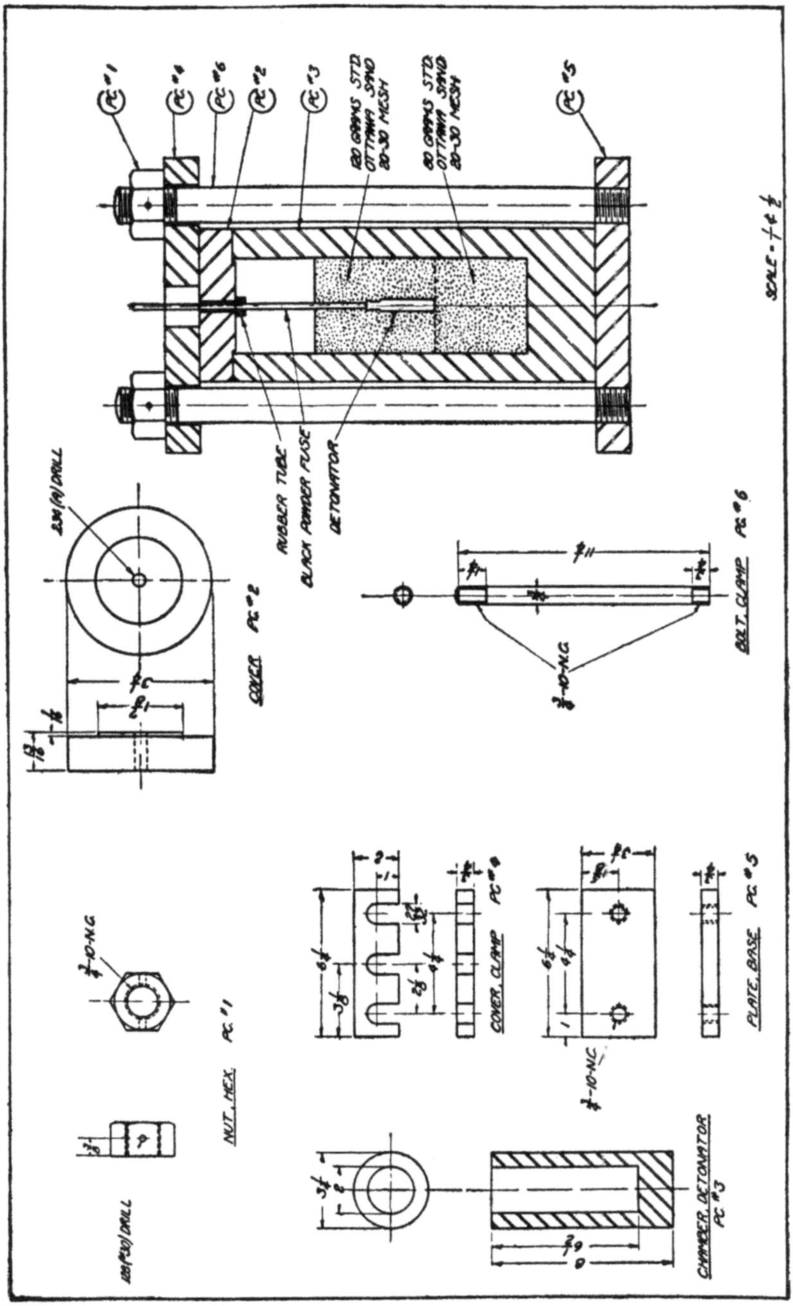
PC #1
PC #4
PC #6
PC #2
PC #3
PC #5
120 GRAMS STD OTTAWA SAND 20-30 MESH
80 GRAMS STD OTTAWA SAND 20-30 MESH
RUBBER TUBE
BLACK POWDER FUSE
DETONATOR
COVER PC #2
BOLT, CLAMP PC #6
NUT, HEX. PC #1
COVER, CLAMP PC #4
PLATE, BASE PC #5
CHAMBER, DETONATOR PC #3

FIGURE 29.

about 1/8 inch long and of such inner diameter that it fits the fuse snugly is slipped over the fuse and adjusted at a point on the fuse in such a manner that when the detonator is in position the rubber will be against the inner side of the bomb cover. The cover is then securely fastened to the bomb, taking care not to displace the cap in the sand. The fuse is lighted and after the explosion has taken place the sand is emptied onto a smooth glazed piece of paper, care being taken to remove completely any sand adhering to the sides of the bomb, or to pieces of the detonator or shell, or burnt fuse. All of the sand is emptied onto the No. 30 Bureau of Standards sand sieve and the amount which passes through after shaking for 2 minutes is weighed. The TNT is considered as having been completely detonated if the average amount of sand passing through the 30-mesh sieve in five trials is not less than 42 grams.

## Section VIII

### AMATOL

                                                              Paragraph
General _____    80
Properties _____    81
Manufacture_____    82
Inspection_____    83

**80. General.**—Amatol is a mixture of ammonium nitrate and TNT. Due to the shortage of toluene during the early stages of the World War, the British Government developed this explosive and adopted it after exhaustive tests as a bursting charge for high-explosive shell. The United States Government shortly after its entrance into the World War and for similar reasons authorized its use as follows: 50/50 for shell from 75 mm. up to and including 4.7 inches; 80/20 for shell from 4.7 inches up to and including 9.2 inches. The ingredients are mixed by weight. The first figure refers to ammonium nitrate, the second to TNT.

**81. Properties.**—Amatol is hygroscopic, insensitive to friction, but can be detonated by severe impact. It has no tendency to form dangerous compounds with metals other than copper. It is more insensitive to explosion by initiators than TNT. 50/50 amatol has approximately the same rate of detonation and strength as TNT, but 80/20 amatol is slightly lower in rate of detonation and brisance. On detonation the ammonium nitrate oxidizes the excess carbon of the TNT with the result that 80/20 amatol produces a white smoke on detonation and 50/50 amatol a smoke less black than straight TNT.

**82. Manufacture.**—*a. 50/50 amatol.*—The ammonium nitrate as received may contain some moisture and must be dried to a moisture content of not more than .25 percent. It may also be found that caking has occurred in the barrels or drums in which it has been shipped. To break up the lumps it is often necessary to first run the material through a crusher, after which it is dried to the proper moisture content. After drying, the material is screened to remove any foreign material with which it may have become contaminated. It is now ready for addition to molten TNT. The speed of adding ammonium nitrate to TNT can be increased greatly if the ammonium nitrate can be added while it is still hot. It must be added at a rate so that no solidification of the molten TNT takes place in the melting kettle. Proportions for use in mixing 50/50 amatol range from 45 percent to 55 percent ammonium nitrate. This variation is permitted to take care of the various granulations, fine material requiring more TNT than coarse material. Temperature of the mixture when it is ready for pouring in the shell is 80° to 85° C.

*b. 80/20 Amatol.*—(1) 80/20 amatol is a plastic mass resembling wet brown sugar and cannot be loaded by the casting method. The principal difficulty experienced with 80/20 amatol is to obtain ammonium nitrate which has proper granulation. With very fine material, plasticity of the mass is such that when loaded density falls below the point desired, namely, not less than 1.38. With coarse material molten TNT is not completely absorbed and a relatively large amount leaks out in the extruding operation which results in a charge of low density. It is therefore essential that granulation be such as to give a mixture which will not permit leaking of TNT and which will be sufficiently plastic to consolidate well from the extruder. It has been found that a mixture of coarse and fine material is the most suitable for this operation. Granulation requirements are through a No. 10 U. S. standard sieve not less than 99.0 percent; through a No. 10 on No. 35, 32 to 48 percent; through a No. 100, 15 to 30 percent.

(2) Preparation of 80/20 amatol is conducted in a mixing kettle having a capacity of about 500 pounds of amatol. The correct amount of ammonium nitrate is added to the kettle and heated to the point where solidification of TNT will not occur. When the ammonium nitrate has been raised to at least 90° C., molten TNT is added and the charge thoroughly mixed for 15 minutes. At the end of this time it is transferred to the extruding machine from which it is forced into the shell by means of a screw working inside of a steel tube. This

machine is counterweighted so that the material is forced into the shell under a definite pressure.

**83. Inspection.**—*a. Raw materials.*—Ammonium nitrate and TNT used in preparation of amatol must conform to U. S. Army specifications governing these materials, as impurities in both have harmful effects on the resulting product. Oily impurities in the TNT will cause exudation or leakage, while impurities in ammonium nitrate such as pyridine, cyanide, etc., will cause formation of gas or frothing, resulting in probable cavitation in the shell. Methods of analysis governing inspection of these materials are given elsewhere in this manual.

*b. Samples.*—Samples should be taken from the mixer while the stirrers are rotated as the TNT and ammonium nitrate have a tendency to segregate. It is desirable to take the sample in an aluminum or thin sheet-iron vessel, a circular piece of stout cardboard being placed in the bottom. To obtain concordant results with duplicate analyses, experience will show that extreme care must be taken with the samples.

*c. Tests.*—(1) *Moisture.*—Dish and dome method: An aluminum dish and dome (cover) is heated for 15 minutes, cooled in the desiccator and weighed. Approximately 5 grams of the sample is added to the dish which is placed on the top of a water oven for 3 hours. After cooling in a desiccator for 20 minutes, the weight is taken. Loss in weight equals moisture present in original sample. A small quantity of TNT sublimes but condenses on the inside of the cover which should be cleaned thoroughly before using in another test.

(2) *TNT.*—Extraction with benzene: A dry filter paper folded so as to leave a small cavity in the center is weighed in a tared weighing bottle. About 2 grams of powdered amatol is placed in the filter paper without removing it from the bottle and the bottle reweighed. The paper and amatol are transferred to a small funnel and washed with approximately 75 cc. hot benzene, adding enough at a time to cover the powder. After about one-half of the benzene has been added the remainder can be poured in rapidly, taking care to wash thoroughly the sides of the filter paper. The filter paper and residue are transferred from the funnel to the top of a steam oven in order to remove the greater portion of the benzene and dried in a tared weighing bottle for 1 hour. Loss in weight equals TNT plus moisture.

(3) *Ammonium nitrate.*—Extraction with water: A known weight, approximately 2 grams, is extracted with 50 cc. hot water at a temperature not less than 85° C. After cooling, the solution is filtered and the process repeated three times with 50 cc., 30 cc., and 20 cc. suc-

cessive quantities of hot water. The combined filtrates are evaporated just to dryness in a tared dish and left in a vacuum desiccator overnight. The residue is rinsed two or three times with anhydrous ether, dried on top of the oven to remove ether vapors, cooled, and weighed. The residue equals ammonium nitrate present in the sample.

## Section IX

## LEAD AZIDE

|  | Paragraph |
|---|---|
| General | 84 |
| Properties | 85 |
| Manufacture | 86 |
| Storage | 87 |
| Inspection | 88 |

**84. General.**—Lead azide was first prepared and identified by Curtius in 1891 and in 1893 Will and Lenze began an investigation of lead azide as a military explosive. About 1910 commercial manufacture of lead azide was started abroad and has continued up to the present time. Since 1931 it has been produced commercially in this country. This commercial lead azide is free from needle crystals having a maximum dimension greater than 0.1 mm.

**85. Properties.**—Lead azide $(PbN_6)$ is an initiating compound used for bringing about detonation of high explosives. It is sensitive to flame but is too insensitive to be used alone where initiation is by impact of a firing pin. Lead azide is practically insoluble in water and its hygroscopicity at 30° C. and 90 percent relative humidity is only 0.03 percent. It is not easily decomposed by heat as shown by surveillance tests where it has been stored for 15 months at 80° C. without any noted impairment in sensitivity or brisance.

**86. Manufacture.**—*a. Formulas.*—Lead azide may be produced according to the following reaction:

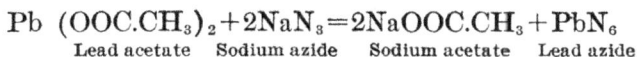

$$Pb\,(OOC.CH_3)_2 + 2NaN_3 = 2NaOOC.CH_3 + PbN_6$$

Lead acetate   Sodium azide   Sodium acetate   Lead azide

Pure sodium azide $(NaN_3)$ may be prepared by converting metallic sodium to sodium amide in a current of ammonia and then treating the sodium amide with nitrous oxide:

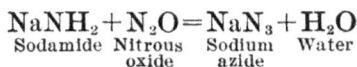

$$NaNH_2 + N_2O = NaN_3 + H_2O$$

Sodamide   Nitrous   Sodium   Water
oxide   azide

The water liberated reacts with one-half of the $NaNH_2$:

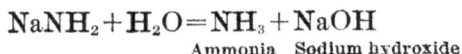

$$NaNH_2 + H_2O = NH_3 + NaOH$$

Ammonia   Sodium hydroxide

The reaction is completed when no more ammonia is evolved. The mixture of sodium azide and sodium hydroxide is separated by recrystallization from water.

*b. Method.*—The conversion of sodium azide to lead azide is carried out in barricaded equipment. A method described by R. Wallbaum is as follows: A 5 percent lead acetate solution is placed in a suitable reaction vessel at room temperature and a 2 percent solution of sodium azide added slowly, the contents of the vessel being stirred constantly. In order to avoid danger of handling pure lead azide it is customary to prepare technical lead azide, 90 to 95 percent pure in granular form. This is accomplished by adding dextrin to the lead solution which produces a yellow-white product with no crystal faces observable under the microscope (50X).

**87. Storage.**—Lead azide is always stored thoroughly saturated with water. It is stored and handled in the same manner as mercury fulminate (see sec. VII). Spilled lead azide may be destroyed by washing floors, benches, etc., with a solution of ammonium acetate.

**88. Inspection.**—*a. Specifications.*—Requirements for lead azide as prescribed in U. S. Army specifications are—

(1) Color, white to buff.

(2) Form, aggregates free from needle-shaped crystals having a maxium dimension greater than 0.1 mm.

(3) Purity, lead content not less than 68.5 percent nor more than 71.15 percent.

(4) Acidity, none.

(5) Solubility, not more that 1.0 percent in cold distilled water.

(6) Sand test: When 0.15 gram of lead azide is used to initiate 0.40 gram of tetryl, not less than 45 grams of sand will be crushed.

*b. Tests.*—Methods prescribed for testing are as follows:

(1) *Color.*—Determined by visual inspection.

(2) *Form.*—Determined by inspection under a microscope, using a magnification of 150. If needle-shaped crystals are observed, their maxium dimension is measured by means of a measuring microscope.

(3) *Purity.*—The sample is dried in a steam oven at 95° C. An accurately weighed portion of approximately 1 gram of the sample is transferred to a 400-cc. beaker. 50 cc. of a saturated solution of ammonium acetate is added and the azide dissolved by stirring and warming. The solution is diluted with 200 cc. of distilled water and heated to boiling. With rapid agitation 10 cc. of a 10 percent solution of potassium dichromate is added slowly. It is digested on a hot plate or steam bath for 1 hour, with frequent stirring. The precipitate of lead

chromate is caught on a tared Gooch crucible, washed with hot distilled water, and the crucible and precipitate are dried for 2 hours at 100° C., cooled in a desiccator, and weighed. Weight of the precipitate in terms of percentage of lead in the sample is calculated:

$$PbCrO_4 \times 0.64109 = Pb$$

(4) *Acidity.*—An accurately weighed portion of approximately 10 grams of the sample dried at 95° C. is transferred to a tared Gooch crucible. It is washed with five 20-cc. portions of cold distilled water which has been boiled prior to the test. Each portion of water is allowed to remain in contact with the azide for 3 minutes. Five drops of methyl orange solution containing 1 gram of methyl orange per liter of solution are added to the filtrate. Development of a red tinge indicates presence of acidity.

(5) *Solubility.*—The crucible and azide from acidity determination are dried to constant weight using a vacuum desiccator or a steam oven having a temperature of 95° C., weighed, and the loss in weight calculated in terms of percentage solubility of the sample.

(6) *Sand test.*—(a) *Loading caps.*—To each of five empty No. 6 blasting caps 0.400±0.001 gram of tetryl complying with Specification No. 50–13–4 is transferred. Each blasting cap is composed of copper, gilding metal, or aluminum, and approximately 1.46 inches long by 0.217 inch inside diameter. With the cap held in a loading block, a plunger 0.20 inch in diameter is inserted in the shell and the tetryl subjected to a pressure of 3,000 pounds per square inch (100 pounds actual load) for 3 minutes. The plunger is removed and 0.150±0.001 gram of dried azide sample is transferred to the shell. The plunger is inserted in the shell and a pressure of 3,000 pounds per square inch applied for 1 minute. The powder train in one end of a piece of miner's fuse 8 or 9 inches long is pricked with a pin. To the pricked end, one of the caps loaded as directed above is crimped, taking care that the end of the fuse is held firmly against the charge in the cap. Crimping is done near the mouth of the cap so as to avoid squeezing the charge.

(b) *Method.*—80±0.1 grams of standard Ottawa sand which passes through a No. 20 Bureau of Standards sand sieve (opening, 0.0335 inch; wire diameter, 0.0165 inch) and is retained on a No. 30 Bureau of Standards sand sieve (opening, 0.0223 inch; wire diameter, 0.0110 inch) are poured into the cavity of the sand test bomb and it is leveled by striking the bomb two or three times. The fuse is inserted through the hole in the cover of the bomb and the cap lowered into the bomb cavity so that it is in the center of the cavity and just touching the sand. 120±0.1 grams more of the sand are poured around the cap and bomb tapped as before to level the sand.

To avoid possible loss of sand caused by the explosion blowing the burned fuse through the hole in the cover, a piece of rubber tubing about ⅛ inch long and of such inner diameter that it fits the fuse snugly is slipped over the fuse and adjusted at a point on the fuse so that the rubber will be against the inner side of the bomb cover when the detonator is in position. The cover is fastened securely to the bomb, taking care not to displace the cap in the sand. The fuze is lighted and after the explosion has taken place, the sand is emptied onto a sheet of smooth glazed paper taking care to remove any sand which may adhere to the side of the bomb, or to pieces of the detonator shell or burnt fuse. All the sand is emptied on the No. 30 Bureau of Standards sand sieve fitted with a pan, and the sand which passes through the sieve after shaking 3 minutes is weighed.

# CHAPTER 3

# BIBLIOGRAPHY

**89. Bibliography.**

Berthelot, "Explosives and Their Power," Translation, Hake and Macnab, John Murray, London.

Buisson, "Problems Des Poudres," P. Juillard, Bul. Soc. Chem. 33, 1905, p. 1172.

Escales, Richard, Dr., "Die Explosivstoffe mist besondere berucksichtigung der Neuren Patente Bearbitet von."

Humphrey, Journal Industrial and Engineering Chemistry, vol 8, November, 1916.

Journal of Industrial and Engineering Chemistry, Analytical Edition, vol. I, No. 1, 1929, p. 49.

Marshall, "Explosives," vol. 1, 1917, pp. 135–136, Blakistons & Co.

Official and Tentative Methods of Analyses of the Association of Official Agricultural Chemists, Second Edition, pp. 464–477.

Tschappat, "Ordnance and Gunnery," 1917, pp. 115, 518, J. Wiley & Sons, N. Y.

# INDEX

| | Paragraphs | Pages |
|---|---|---|
| Acid, picric | 56–61 | 99–104 |
| Amatol | 80 | 124 |
|     Inspection | 83 | 126 |
|     Manufacture | 82 | 125 |
|     Properties | 81 | 124 |
| Ammonium picrate (explosive D) | 50 | 94 |
|     Inspection | 54 | 96 |
|     Manufacture | 52 | 95 |
|     Properties | 51 | 94 |
|     Storage | 55 | 98 |
|     Use | 53 | 96 |
| Bibliography | 89 | 131 |
| Cannon powders, FNH and NH | 17 | 34 |
| Colloid, formation of | 12 | 20 |
| Cotton, raw, purification | 9 | 6 |
| Definitions | 1 | 1 |
| DuPont nitrometer | 29 | 61 |
| Explosive D (ammonium picrate) | 50–55 | 94–99 |
| Explosives: | | |
|     Action | 3 | 3 |
|     Classification | 2 | 2 |
|     Composition | 5 | 4 |
|     Definition | 1 | 1 |
|     High, military | 40, 41 | 84 |
|     Nitrostarch | 62–67 | 105–111 |
|     Use | 4 | 3 |
| Inspection of— | | |
|     Amatol | 83 | 126 |
|     Ammonium picrate (explosive D) | 54 | 96 |
|     Lead azide | 88 | 128 |
|     Mercury fulminate | 79 | 120 |
|     Nitrostarch explosives | 67 | 109 |
|     Picric acid | 60 | 102 |
|     Powder: | | |
|         Black | 38 | 80 |
|         Smokeless | 27 | 52 |
|     Tetryl | 73 | 113 |
|     Trinitrotoluene (TNT) | 48 | 91 |
| Lead azide | 84 | 127 |
|     Inspection | 88 | 128 |
|     Manufacture | 86 | 127 |
|     Properties | 85 | 127 |
|     Storage | 87 | 128 |
| Military high explosives: | | |
|     Manufacture | 41 | 84 |
|     Requirements | 40 | 84 |

|  | Paragraphs | Pages |
|---|---|---|
| Mercury fulminate | 74 | 115 |
| Inspection | 79 | 120 |
| Manufacture | 75 | 116 |
| Properties | 76 | 117 |
| Storage | 78 | 119 |
| Use | 77 | 119 |
| Nitration | 10 | 9 |
| Trinitrotoluene (TNT) | 45 | 86 |
| Nitrocellulose testing | 30 | 63 |
| Nitrometer, DuPont | 29 | 61 |
| Nitrostarch explosives | 62 | 105 |
| Inspection | 67 | 109 |
| Manufacture | 63 | 105 |
| Properties | 64 | 106 |
| Storage | 66 | 108 |
| Use | 65 | 108 |
| Picric acid | 56 | 99 |
| Inspection | 60 | 102 |
| Manufacture | 58 | 100 |
| Properties | 57 | 99 |
| Storage | 61 | 104 |
| Use | 59 | 101 |
| Powder: |  |  |
| Black | 35 | 77 |
| Inspection | 38 | 80 |
| Manufacture | 36 | 78 |
| Packing | 37 | 79 |
| Storage | 39 | 83 |
| Cannon, FNH and NH | 17 | 34 |
| Double base | 33 | 75 |
| E. C | 34 | 76 |
| Smokeless: |  |  |
| Cotton, raw, purification for | 9 | 6 |
| Form | 7 | 5 |
| Grains: |  |  |
| Dimension control | 20 | 42 |
| Form and size | 19 | 36 |
| Granulation | 18 | 36 |
| Historical sketch of | 6 | 4 |
| Inspection | 27 | 52 |
| Instability, causes | 23 | 47 |
| Manufacturing processes | 8 | 6 |
| Blending | 16 | 32 |
| Drying | 15 | 30 |
| Graining and cutting | 13 | 25 |
| Shipment | 26 | 51 |
| Stability | 21 | 46 |
| Tests | 22 | 46 |
| Stabilizers | 24 | 48 |
| Storage | 21, 25 | 46, 49 |
| Testing | 22, 31 | 46, 68 |

| | Paragraphs | Pages |
|---|---|---|
| Propellants, compound | 32 | 74 |
| Pyrocotton purification | 11 | 14 |
| Raw material testing | 28 | 52 |
| Smokeless powder | 6–31 | 4–74 |
| Solvent recovery | 14 | 26 |
| Storage: | | |
|     Ammonium picrate (explosive D) | 55 | 98 |
|     Lead azide | 87 | 128 |
|     Mercury fulminate | 78 | 119 |
|     Nitrostarch explosives | 66 | 108 |
|     Picric acid | 61 | 104 |
|     Powder: | | |
|         Black | 39 | 83 |
|         Smokeless | 21, 25 | 46, 49 |
|     Tetryl | 72 | 113 |
|     Trinitrotoluene (TNT) | 49 | 93 |
| Testing: | | |
|     Nitrocellulose | 30 | 63 |
|     Raw materials | 28 | 52 |
|     Smokeless powder | 22, 31 | 46, 68 |
| Tetryl | 68 | 111 |
|     Inspection | 73 | 113 |
|     Manufacture | 69 | 111 |
|     Properties | 70 | 112 |
|     Storage and handling | 72 | 113 |
|     Use | 71 | 112 |
| Trinitrotoluene (TNT) | 42 | 84 |
|     Inspection | 48 | 91 |
|     Manufacture | 44 | 86 |
|     Nitration | 45 | 86 |
|     Properties | 43 | 85 |
|     Purification | 46 | 89 |
|     Storage | 49 | 93 |
|     Use | 47 | 90 |

[A. G. 062.11 (6–18–40).]

By order of the Secretary of War:

G. C. MARSHALL,
*Chief of Staff.*

Offcial:

E. S. ADAMS,
*Major General,*
*The Adjutant General.*

©2022 Periscope Film LLC
All Rights Reserved
978-1-940453-69-9
www.PeriscopeFilm.com

www.ingramcontent.com/pod-product-compliance
Lightning Source LLC
Chambersburg PA
CBHW070105070426
42448CB00038B/1723